# A Century of Preservation

A Pictorial and Historical Narrative
of the Sempervirens Club and the Sempervirens Fund

# *The Sempervirens Story:*

## A Century of Preserving California's Ancient Redwood Forest 1900 — 2000

BY
### Willie Yaryan
AND
### Denzil & Jennie Verardo

Sempervirens Fund
Los Altos, California

Deer, Big Basin Redwoods State Park.
*Photo: Cal Yeates, Sempervirens Fund Collection*

# Contents

Looking West from Big Basin Redwoods State Park.    *Photo: Alexander Lowry, Sempervirens Fund Collection.*

# FOREWORD

by

Claude "Tony" Look

The first organization to preserve California redwoods, the Sempervirens Club, led by Andrew P. Hill, was founded in 1900.

In 1968 —led by Doris Leonard, Dorothy Varian, and George Collins— collectively known as Conservation Associates, with the additional assistance of Richard Leonard Esq. The organization's name was changed from the Sempervirens Club to the Sempervirens Fund.

The Sempervirens Fund was founded on the strong leadership of Conservation Associates and the historic work of the Sempervirens Club. The Sempervirens Fund's officers pledged to complete and connect California's first state park, Big Basin, with the spectacular Castle Rock State Park. The connection was accomplished by the building of the "Skyline-to-the-Sea Trail" in 1969.

With nearly 20,000 acres preserved since 1900, the story continues today; as redwood forests are being challenged by both the logging industry and the modern real estate boom.

We dedicate this very important story of the preservation of the Coast Redwoods to Conservation Associates and Richard Leonard, to all of our donors who have made it happen, and to our advisors in the State park system who have placed their trust in what we did and are doing.

We especially want to thank the Sempervirens Fund staff — past and present.

The Sempervirens Fund, Los Altos, CA 94023

Library of Congress Control Number:  00-131538
ISBN 0-9701178-0-9

Cover photograph: Doug Yule, Private Collection

Willie Yaryan donates any copyright interests and royalties
Which may accrue and any other possessory interest in The
Sempervirens Story to the Sempervirens Fund.

Denzil and Jennie Verardo donate any copyright interests,
royalties which may accrue, actual value of time and materials
used to produce and author, and any other possessory interest
in The Sempervirens Story to the Sempervirens Fund.

The Sempervirens Fund, Drawer BE, Los Altos, CA 94023

# Acknowledgements

The authors thank the following individuals and institutions whose courtesy and assistance made the production of this work both easier and more complete:

Rachel McKay at the Santa Cruz Museum of Art and History; Charlene Duval at the Sourisseau Academy, San Jose State University; Paula Jabloner with the History Museums of San Jose; authors Carolyn De Vries and Joe Engbeck; and Richard Wilson of the California Department of Parks and Recreation. Without Tony Look this work would not have been possible, nor would it have been produced. Verl Clausen added both insight and perspective to his years as Executive Director of the Sempervirens Fund and Ellie Giffen was tireless in the work of proofing the copy. The Bancroft Library, California State Library, McHenry Library at the University of California, Santa Cruz, Orradre Library at the University of Santa Clara, and the Stanford University Library provided critical research resources.

Sunlight filtering through the morning fog, Big Basin Redwoods State Park.  *Photo: Sempervirens Fund Collection*

# I.

## The  Thickest, Tallest, Straightest Trees. . .

*(As we headed north, there were) the thickest, tallest, and straightest trees we had ever seen.*

Frey Francisco Palou, 1769
(with the Portola expedition)

**M**embers of the conifer or "cone-bearing" family of trees, redwoods are the largest and tallest living plant species. They have been on earth at least 130 million years, ranking them among the most ancient of trees. Their range covered vast areas of the globe. Once numbering approximately forty species, redwoods have now dwindled to three species — two in California and one in China.

The coast redwood *(Sequoia sempervirens)* which can grow to a height of over 350 feet, is found in a narrow 450 mile long strip along California's coast from south of Big Sur to just north of the California-Oregon border. Despite agitation by the British to label them *Wellingtonia* and by some Americans to call them *Washingtonia*, this species was named after Chief Sequoyah, the developer of the Cherokee alphabet. Coast redwoods may reach an age of 2,200 years, and one is the tallest tree in the world.

The giant sequoia *(Sequoia gigantea)* of California's Sierra Nevada range is shorter than the coast redwood, but is among the oldest living of the three Sequoia species, attaining an age up to 3,600 years. Only the much smaller bristlecone pine lives longer, reaching 4,000 years or more. The dawn redwood, a native of south central China, was identified by its fossil remains in 1941, long before botanists became aware that the tree still exists.

It is thought that Native Americans avoided the redwood forests except for rituals. The forests were home to grizzly bears. Tribal peoples seem to have chosen to shun that risk and remain among the oak trees along the coast or in the inland valleys where their principle food, the acorn, could be found.

Europeans discovered the giant redwood trees that grew along the coast in the fall of 1769, when the Portola expedition traveled north from Baja California searching for Monterey Bay. Camping on the Pajaro River near present-day Watsonville, they found the "thickest, tallest and straightest trees they had ever seen". The Spaniards named them *palo colorado* — "red wood". Failing to recognize their intended objective, the group pushed farther north and camped for several days at the mouth of Waddell Creek, which flows from the Big Basin, before returning south to Baja California. The *Sequoia gigantea* of the Sierra Nevada, would not be discovered by Europeans until eighty years later. With discovery, would eventually come the exploitation of both species.

The first felling of a coast redwood in California should have been an epochal event. However, the fellers involved most probably lacked the sophistication to understand the significance of their action. Trees that were young when the Roman Empire began, were unceremoniously cut down for crude houses and fence rails. Although forests were logged primarily for local construction during the Spanish and Mexican occupation of California, expansion of the logging industry had its roots in this period. Missionized Native Americans were trained for the task by the padres. In 1791, Ohlones from Mission Santa Clara cut down the first redwoods in the Santa Cruz area for timber and shingles to build Mission Santa Cruz. A flurry of logging operations were set off by Governor Jose Joaquin Arrillaga's 1793 orders to strengthen Spain's coastal presidios against possible foreign aggression from Russia or Britain, as they expanded their exploration and colonization efforts. British explorer George Vancouver had taken redwood branches and cones back to Europe in the late 1700's. In 1804, redwood would be introduced to the new United States when a ship, the *Hazard* from Rhode Island, was repaired with redwood while in port at San Francisco. Redwood was also being shipped to timber-starved Peru from Monterey before 1815.

In the 1830's and 1840's, the Santa Cruz Mountains became the refuge for English and American sailors who had jumped ship in Monterey Bay and who found an easy source of income in logging. The boards were cut with whipsaws, trimmed in shallow pits and hauled to the coast for sale and shipping. Local redwoods were delivered to Yankee trader Thomas Larkin in Monterey for transport to Hawaii, where redwood was used to build the first missionary churches, as well as to China and Chile. Larkin was the first in California to use redwood to build a two-story house. That home stands today as a historic monument in Monterey. This achievement was quickly and widely imitated, and Larkin dominated the California lumber industry for nearly fifteen years. Lumber, like cow hides which were shipped to New England to be made into shoes, was a handy substitute for money in Mexican Alta California. By the 1840's, there were three water-driven sawmills operating in the San Lorenzo Valley which would put the whipsawyers out of business.

During the Gold Rush of the late 1840's and 1850's, redwood was in big demand for mine timbers and, as trains came west, for railroad ties. By 1884, there were twenty-eight sawmills on the coast south of San Francisco and in the San Lorenzo Valley region, cutting thirty-four million board feet of lumber per year, not including vast quantities of shingles, shakes, posts, railroad ties, and cord wood. Before the turn of the next century, most of the redwood in easily accessible regions of the Santa Cruz Mountains between San Francisco and Monterey had been cut down. Loggers had begun to move north to Mendocino, Humboldt, and Del Norte Counties, as well as to Washington and Oregon, where the trees still seemed inexhaustible.

After statehood in 1850, California's land was practically free for the asking. Popular sentiment was against regulating logging and a series of acts by Congress made it easy and profitable to acquire land for timber. These included the Timber Culture Act of 1872 and, the Free Timber Act and Timber and Stone Act of 1878. Each action by the federal government also provided potential loopholes for corruption and permitted concentration of redwood forests in the hands of huge logging companies. In 1901 when charges were made that land speculators had bought up 17,000 acres of Big Basin land with the intention of selling it back to the State after the park bill was approved for the price of $100 an acre, the *Boulder Creek Mountain Echo* editorialized that:

*all the best lands in the Big Basin were secured by land speculators thirty-five years ago when they were located by Messrs. Chapman, Moore and Templeton, immediately on the heels of the Government surveyors in 1866. It is only recently that these lands came into the possession of practical lumbermen, who a year or so ago began working the timber into marketable products and who still have their men and machinery on the ground for this purpose.*

Of the many lumber mills built in the Santa Cruz area during this period, was one built in 1862, the year the Homestead Act made 160 acres of federal land in the west available to any settler who claimed it. William Waddell, who had come to California in 1851 and had already built three mills to the south, constructed this new mill five miles inland from the ocean in an area that was called the Big Basin, at the junction of two forks of a creek he named for himself. Waddell, a cousin of the founder of the Pony Express, also constructed a wharf and a horse tramway to the ocean from his mill to carry lumber to waiting ships. With Waddell's untimely death from injuries inflicted by a grizzly bear in 1875, lumbering in that area sharply declined.

On the eastern flank of Ben Lomond Mountain in the year Waddell died, railroad tracks were pushed north from Santa Cruz, and an eighteen-mile flume was constructed to carry logs south from Waterman Gap to the town of Felton where the flume and train met. Within ten years, the train had replaced the flume, winding up to Boulder Creek and beyond. However, a projected rail line to Pescadero which would have skirted the Big Basin and opened it up more fully to logging never materialized. Dreams of a coast railroad that would have opened up the lower Waddell Creek area were a casualty of the 1906 earthquake

An eighteen-mile flume was constructed to carry logs south from Waterman Gap to the town of Felton.

*Photo: History San Jose Collection*

which caused landslides and destroyed the north coast road.

There were four distinct periods in the lumbering history of the Santa Cruz Mountains redwoods, defined by their technology for logging and milling. Prior to 1842, lumber was created by hand-sawing in pits and limited logging was the rule. From 1842 until 1875, lumber mills were water-powered, and logging was ox-assisted. From 1876 until 1905, steam-powered sawmills, high-speed circular saws, and ox and other low-powered logging were the methods utilized. After 1905, modern logging techniques began to be employed. The activities of the earliest lumbering period changed the appearance and composition of the virgin forest only slightly, while modern logging has produced the most striking changes in the landscape. Each advance in technology, from sawpits to water to steam to rail, was more expensive and demanded a greater return on investment.

In 1879, train service had been established between Oakland and Santa Cruz via Felton, and financial control of the rail line was soon taken over by the Southern Pacific Railroad. By 1885, passenger and freight trains had pushed north from Felton to Boulder Creek, and logging of the San Lorenzo River

watershed began in earnest. Depending on the source quoted, Boulder Creek became the second or the fourth largest lumber-shipping point in California. On one night alone, a seventy-three car freight train loaded with logs left Boulder Creek for Felton. By the 1890's, the dozen miles between Boulder Creek and Waterman Gap had been clear-cut. The *Boulder Creek Mountain Echo* described the condition of the San Lorenzo River Valley north of town:

*Throughout its entire length of about ten miles the timber has been cut out and for the most part the denuded country presents a scene of utter desolation. Where only a few years ago stood the beautiful and almost unbroken primeval forest, the joy of the camper and the sportsman, there is now only a waste of brush land, fast becoming an almost impenetrable jungle. Private roads are being discontinued because there is no longer material to pass over them and even the county roads are becoming impassable because the land has been rendered almost worthless for taxation and there can be, as an inevitable consequence, but little public moneys available to repair them. In so far as business is concerned this valley is fast becoming a solitude and a cipher.*

Loggers then focused on the Waddell Creek watershed in Big Basin as the only virgin timber remaining in the Santa Cruz Mountains.

The steam donkeys pulled the huge logs to staging areas where the oxen teams could drag them down hill to the steam powered saw mills.

*Photo: History San Jose Collection*

One of the many logging mills in the Santa Cruz Mountains at the turn of the last century.

*Photo: Sempervirens Fund Collection*

# II.

## Early Preservation Cries

*I feel most emphatically that we should not turn a tree which was old when the first Egyptian conqueror penetrated the Valley of the Euphrates into shingles.*

**President Theodore Roosevelt**
**Santa Cruz, 1903**

Since the Native Americans, Spaniards, and Mexicans had essentially left the redwoods alone, there was no perceived need for conservation until well into the nineteenth century, when logging had become a profitable business enterprise. As early as 1852, Assemblymember Henry A. Crabb of San Joaquin County asked the California legislature to secure into public ownership all of the state's redwood forest lands. His resolution, which did not pass, was clearly a reaction to market abuses:

*WHEREAS there is good reason to fear that the rapidly increasing demand for (timber) will soon exhaust the supply if precautionary measures in regard thereto are not adopted at an early day, therefore*

*BE IT RESOLVED that...the settlement and occupation of all public lands upon which Red Wood (sic) is growing shall be prohibited and the Red Wood (sic) timber shall be declared to be the common property of the citizens of California for their private use and benefit provided such timber shall not be made the subject of trade and traffic.*

In 1864, George Perkins Marsh published his popular book *Man and Nature,* which warned against the detrimental effects of forest destruction on climate and water supply. In the following year, the annual report of the Federal Commissioner of Agriculture contained ominous warnings against forest devastation. By 1866, the General Land Office in the U.S. Department of the Interior predicted that the entire timber supply of the country could be exhausted within

fifty years. In the 1870's, the American Association for the Advancement of Science pushed for government intervention to preserve forests. By 1879, U.S. Secretary of the Interior Carl Shurtz, had asked Congress to set aside a coast redwood preserve of at least two townships, about 46,000 acres.

During this same 1870's period, Irish immigrant Tom Maddock was lured to California by the promotional literature of Tom Scott who owned the Texas and Pacific Railroad. Maddock had milked cows in Marin County before coming to Boulder Creek to work as a teamster hauling wood. In the summer of 1877, after the flume for floating lumber from the mountains to the ocean put him out of business, Tom Maddock built a squatter's cabin in Big Basin, on land that belonged to the same Tom Scott whose literature had brought Maddock west. He harvested tan oak bark for the leather tanneries of Santa Cruz and Santa Clara; cut redwoods into ties, fence posts, and pickets and staves for tanning vats; and logged madrone for gunpowder which was produced near Felton and which was needed in the mines. In 1882, Scott's original claim was forfeited and Maddock was able to secure 160 acres of forest land for the filing fee of $7.50. In 1883, he built a new cabin from a single redwood tree on the banks of Scott Creek. Maddock's cabin remained standing well into the present century and the site has been preserved as part of Big Basin Redwoods State Park.

In 1886, over the mountains north of Maddock's cabin, Ralph Sidney Smith, editor of the *Redwood City Times and Gazette,* began writing about the wisdom of preserving a portion of California's unique redwood forest. Smith felt that this preservation would have value not only in creating a tourist attraction of economic importance, but for scientific research purposes, and as a long-term investment for the inspiration and education of present and future citizens. This was only a year after the railroad had penetrated the heart of the Santa Cruz Mountains, making large-scale logging possible. "I want a portion of this forest saved from destruction forever", he wrote in an editorial which was reprinted in San Francisco, San Jose, and Santa Cruz. There were some who said that Smith's zeal on behalf of a forest reserve was stimulated by the desire of the Spring Valley Water Company, which supplied water to San Francisco, to secure a permanent cover for their Pescadero watershed. Smith could not really be called a nature preservationist, for his vision of the mountaintop reserve was decidedly development-oriented. He wrote:

*The region lends itself readily to picturesque road-building, and drives and bridal paths might be made to command a panorama of unexampled variety.*

*I want its savage beauty enhanced by the skill of enlightened forestry. I want glades opened, hotels built, camping grounds laid out, game preserves stocked with trout, and the big etcetera which wealth working harmoniously with nature may create and perpetuate.*

The journalist's proposal for a 20,000 acre park in the upper portions of the Pescadero and Butano Creek watersheds, which he said could be purchased for no more than $15 an acre, was enthusiastically endorsed by Bay Area newspapers. According to the *San Francisco Chronicle*:

*(W)e know of no way in which the public money could be better invested, or which would return a better income for all future time. We must not be construed as meaning that the park would pay an annual interest on the investment into the state treasure; but there are other kinds of income besides interest. Golden Gate Park is not a paying institution in the ordinary acceptation of the term, but it would be hard to convince a San Franciscan that the city has ever invested any money to better purpose than there. Yosemite, Yellowstone Park, Niagara — none of them pay money dividends yet each is worth untold wealth to the nation.*

Writing in the *Oakland Tribune* in 1887, popular writer and satirist Ambrose Bierce, envisioned such a preserve as "a resort for pleasure seekers" and concluded that it would prevent the destruction of "that really 'noble savage,' the redwood". Popular precedents in the public's mind for preserving Big Basin were Yosemite (1864), Yellowstone (1872), Niagara Falls (1885), and Golden Gate Park (1887). Smith's plan was supported by former California Governor and U.S. Senator, Leland Stanford; William H. Jordan, Speaker of the California State Assembly; and noted poet Joaquin Miller, among others. Smith later recognized that Big Basin would be a better site for a park: "The rugged grandeur of its hills, the dense growth and size of its forests, equal anything in this county". He organized special expeditions for influential people to view the trees in Big Basin. They should be protected, he said, because of their unique beauty which should not be in private hands. Smith also argued that Big Basin was important because of its closeness to population centers. At the same time he said logging would be unprofitable there because of the inaccessibility of the trees. This first campaign for preservation of the Big Basin was cut short on November 19, 1887, when Smith was shot in the back and killed by a man whose business ethics he had criticized in print. Only ten days before his death, Smith had taken Abbott Kinney and James Buttner, two members of the California State Board of Forestry, into the mountains. The *Santa Cruz Surf* commented that the party was "enthusiastic in their expressions in favor of the proposed reserve, and will recommend that a tract of several thousand acres be set aside...The movement is certainly a wise one and will meet the endorsement of every one who has a spark of romance in his composition".

The movement to create a park in Big Basin was revived two years later when a retired military man, Captain Ferdinand Lee Clark, proposed that 1,300 acres be set aside as a game preserve and "great redwood park". In an article in the *Santa Cruz Surf*, he wrote that "the place will be swarming with hunters and fishers ". Disputes over land titles forced Clark to give up his idea for a game preserve, but he continued to write articles in the *San Francisco Chronicle* and *San Jose Mercury* encouraging recreational use of the area.

While John Muir, and the Sierra Club he had founded in 1892, directed efforts at preservation in the Sierra, notably Yosemite and the Mariposa Grove of Big Trees, one of the first detailed proposals to preserve coast redwoods came from Sierra Club member William Dudley, a professor of botany at Stanford

University. At a Sierra Club forum and in an article in the Club bulletin during late 1895 and early 1896, Dudley reported his field work had convinced him that the two million acres of redwoods that once stretched for 500 miles along the coastal hills of northern California and southern Oregon were disappearing at a rate that threatened extinction of the ancient groves. Dudley's friend Charles Wing, a professor of civil engineering at Stanford, had accompanied him in the exploration of Big Basin and mapping of the Big Basin area. By 1898, Dudley determined that most of the finest redwood stands in the public domain had either been decimated or sold to lumber companies. The best way to secure a redwood park, he reasoned, was to purchase it from private owners. He felt that the most promising site for such a park was in the Big Basin. Stanford University briefly considered purchasing acreage there for scientific research, but the price was more than the school was willing to pay. Later Timothy Hopkins, adopted son of railroad mogul Mark Hopkins, gave the school 5,000 acres of land in the adjoining Butano watershed. Stanford University would sell that property to timber interests.

By 1900, the threat to redwoods in the Santa Cruz mountains was becoming obvious. "It is a case of now or never with the Big Basin, the last possible reservation of redwoods", wrote an editorial columnist in the *Santa Cruz Surf*. The March 1900 editorial continued:

*Its peculiar topography and distance from transportation preserved the tract in question from the early onslaughts upon the redwoods, and here within forty miles of San Francisco, as the bird flies, is a bit of forest as pristine as "the perfect world by Adam trod," and whose trees cast broad shadows before Rome was built...The timber cutters commenced encroaching on its limits last year. This summer they will do more mischief, and in two years, the region instead of possessing Edenic aspects, will be worse than a Sahara.*

Redwood preservation was in the air in California. In January 1900, San Francisco newspapers had announced that the Calaveras grove of Sierra big trees had been sold to a Wisconsin lumberman. A group of California clubwomen, under the leadership of Laura White, president of the California Club in San Francisco, quickly began a campaign to have the grove set aside in a forest preserve by the

U.S. Congress. Two months later, a resolution was passed and signed by President McKinley to purchase the trees.

The Big Basin redwoods were in private hands and loggers were poised at forest's edge for their destruction. To prevent that, a catalyst was needed to fully ignite latent sentiment for their preservation.

Meeting between oxen and Model T Ford
on the Saratoga Toll Road.

*Photograph taken by Mrs. Stanley Smith of Los Gatos.
Courtesy of Ken Robinson, Private Collection*

The Sempervirens Club in 1904.    *Photo: Andrew P. Hill, Sempervirens Fund Collection*

# III.

## Save the Redwoods!

*Man's work, if destroyed, man may again replace. God's work, God alone can re-create. Accede, then, to the prayers of the people. Save this forest. Save it now.*

**Delphin Delmas, 1902**

In the fall of 1899, a fire in redwoods behind Wrights Station near Felton had been extinguished with wine from a local vineyard. A British publication, The *Wide World Magazine*, commissioned C.F. Holder, President of the California Academy of Sciences, to write an article about it. Holder asked Andrew P. Hill, a well-known artist and photographer from San Jose, for photographs of large coast redwoods to illustrate the story. Hill traveled by train to Welch's Big Trees Grove, a privately-owned park in Felton which is now part of Henry Cowell State Park. He requested permission to photograph the ancient redwood trees from park owner Joseph Welch. Welch refused unless Hill paid him, and Hill returned empty-handed to San Jose. In their 1927 book, *The Acquisition of California Redwood Park*, Frank and Florence Hill recounted that Andrew Hill had felt a little angry, and somewhat disgusted…

*these trees, because of their size and antiquity, were among the natural wonders of the world, and should be saved for posterity. I said to myself, 'I will start a campaign immediately to make a public park of this place.' I argued that as I had been furnishing illustrations for a number of writers, whom I knew quite well, that here was a latent force which, when awakened to a noble cause, would immediately respond, and perhaps arouse the press of the whole country. Thus was born my idea of saving the redwoods.*

While perhaps embellished, the story does mark the beginning of the successful campaign to preserve a remnant of the redwoods in the Santa Cruz Mountains. Hill convinced San Jose poet, attorney, and later judge, John E.

Richards to write articles about the plight of the redwoods for the *San Jose Mercury*. Hill also persuaded noted author Josephine Clifford McCrackin, whose home had been destroyed in the Wrights fire, to write about the preservation efforts for the *Santa Cruz Sentinel* and regional publications such as *Out West*, *Western Field*, and *Overland Monthly*. In a March 7, 1900 letter to the *Santa Cruz Sentinel* headlined "SAVE THE TREES", Mrs. McCrackin described Welch's action in wanting money to photograph the trees as "utterly un-American" and she added that:

*it is un-Californian. And while I raise my feeble voice in protest against the selfishness that would debar others from looking at and enjoying one of God's greatest works merely because to this one man fell the piece of earth on which stand these trees, I beseech the people of this county and our neighbor counties, indeed the people of all our State, to unite their voice with mine and make it loud enough, and strong enough, to reach our legislators and lawmakers, so that they may secure to the ownership of the public another one of those wonderful redwood groves that are the admiration, the envy of the whole civilized world.*

The letter was signed, "An Old Californian". According to John Richards, hers "was the first voice…to raise the rallying cry, 'Save the Redwoods,' which was our slogan". An editorial in the competitive *Santa Cruz Surf* by Arthur A. Taylor, its pint-sized but feisty editor, echoed McCrackin's call and said that since Congress was considering the preservation of the Big Trees of Calaveras in the Sierra, it seemed an opportune time "for the revival of the agitation instigated some years ago in behalf of a redwood preserve".

Hill encouraged the Boards of Trade of both Santa Cruz and San Jose to pass resolutions asking Congress to purchase coast redwood trees for a public park. John F. Coope of the

**First Committee on Saving the Redwoods, May 1, 1900, Stanford University.**
*(Left to Right)* Professor J. Henry Senger, David Starr Jordan, Dr. William Dudley, F. W. Billings,
James McNaughton, John Q. Packard, William T. Jeter, John E. Richards, Carrie Stevens Walter,
Albert Stillman, Professor Charles Wing, John Montgomery, Rufus L. Green.

*Photo: Andrew P. Hill, Sempervirens Fund Collection*

Santa Cruz group urged Hill to call a public meeting. Coope was a wine maker and part-owner, along with his father-in-law F. W. Billings and millionaire John Q. Packard, of the Big Creek Power Company which was located just south of the Waddell Creek watershed. Coope had recently helped form the Board of Trade, a predecessor of the city's Chamber of Commerce. In March 1900, at the Board's first meeting, Coope, its elected secretary said:

> *that what the city needs is a waking up...The trade should be improved by having people of the county who are trading elsewhere to do their purchasing in Santa Cruz. We should find some kind of amusements for visitors...By careful advertising a large amount of tourist travel could be diverted to Santa Cruz.*

Coope was a major organizer of early explorations of Big Basin. He provided horse-drawn carriages for visitors to take them to see the redwoods, and paid for their meals and hotel accommodations in Boulder Creek. What was good for the redwoods would, he presumed, be good for Santa Cruz business as well.

Andrew Hill, who had worked for Stanford University President David Starr Jordan photographing his horses, contacted Jordan to help arrange a meeting of influential people who could help the preservation cause. It was held in

the Stanford University library on May 1, 1900. Prior to this gathering, Coope had relayed to Hill that Charles Anderson, a Santa Cruz physician and naturalist, suggested Big Basin as a better location for the park because it covered a larger area and the trees themselves were bigger than those in the Felton grove. "As your enthusiasm is for these smaller trees, so will it grow in proportion to the size, the grandeur and the vastness of those in the Big Basin", Anderson promised. At the Stanford meeting, Hill learned that botanist William Dudley and other university scientists had already explored Big Basin. They had completed maps and a survey of the area, and were enthusiastic about a public park there.

Dudley had been a colleague of David Starr Jordan at Cornell University and was one of a coterie of scientists brought to the campus by Jordan. He had soon become interested in native flora and studied sequoia trees both in the Santa Cruz Mountains and in the Sierra. A founding member of the Sierra Club, he wrote a "Forestry Notes" column in the group's bulletin for many years. Dudley was a friend of Gifford Pinchot, founder of scientific forestry in the United States. He believed that professional foresters could help prevent the wanton destruction of California's redwoods. For Professor Dudley, "the semi-tropical luxuriance" of the redwood forest in Big Basin, "is beyond anything I have seen in all the splendid woods of our coast".

At the Stanford meeting, a surveying committee was appointed, headed by Andrew Hill and Carrie Stevens Walter of the San Jose Woman's Club. Mrs. Walter was an independent woman who had raised her family while her husband worked a Sierra mining claim. She wrote poetry which was published in *Sunset* and in *Golden Era*, a literary magazine in San Francisco, as well as travel articles for local booster publications. She had also edited her own publication, *The Santa Clara*, which featured photography by Hill. Two weeks after the Stanford meeting, the two journeyed to Big Basin with a party that included Mrs. Walter's friend and fellow clubwoman Louise Jones; Coope and Packard from the Santa Cruz Board of Trade; Charles Wesley Reed of the San Francisco Board of Supervisors, who was also a lawyer specializing in water issues; and two San Jose sportsmen, Roley Kooser, whose father had once been a part owner of the *Santa Cruz Sentinel*, and William W. Richards. Their host on the trip was Henry L. Middleton, whose lumber conglomerate had recently purchased much of the land in Big Basin. Middleton liked the idea of selling his land to the state rather than cutting the trees on it. He provided a guide and cook for the three-day "tramp". Although she was not in attendance, Josephine Clifford McCrackin wrote of the outing, "Mr. Middleton was

dragged, willy-nilly, along with the camping party, and held as friendly hostage while his woodchoppers cut trails in any direction that was suggested. For the first time the extent of the Basin was fully realized, and the value of the watercourses, the Waddell, the Gazos, the Pescadero Creek, the Butano, all taking their sources here. Days were spent in exploration; and before the party went back to civilization... Middleton had become inoculated with the spirit of this redwood-saving crowd".

On May 18, 1900, while sitting around the campfire on the banks of Sempervirens Creek, at the foot of the long granite hill called Slippery Rock, Andrew Hill suggested the formation of an organization to preserve the Big Basin. Coope offered the name, "Sempervirens Club", and a hat was passed for the collection of $32 to start their campaign. Charles Wesley Reed was elected President and a variety of notables were appointed honorary Vice Presidents. "Save the Redwoods" was adopted as the Club's motto. Three specific objectives were set: to save the redwoods for posterity; to save the trees and many species of fauna in the area for scientific study; and to create a park for all people to enjoy.

During the summer and fall of 1900, the campaign gathered momentum. Support was obtained from the Native Sons and Native Daughters of California, the Sierra Club, regional chapters of the Game and Fish

The Jupiter, a 4-4-0 wood burner similar to the ones that operated on the narrow gauge tracks from Santa Cruz, that met the flume from Waterman Gap at the town of Felton, circa 1875.     *Photo: Covello and Covello Historical Collection*

Protective Association, the San Jose Cross Country Club, the San Jose Woman's Club, and the California Pioneers of Santa Clara County. Resolutions endorsing a redwood park were obtained from national groups such as the American Association for the Advancement of Science, the American Forestry Association, and the Society for the Promotion of Agriculture. Unlike his Sierra Club colleague John Muir, William Dudley called for support from federal foresters to help manage the proposed park, a move calculated to win support from national Forestry Chief Pinchot, as well as the American Forestry Association. Henry Middleton offered the group a one year option on 14,000 acres in the Big Basin area.

After a trip to the Basin that summer, founding Sempervirens Club member and the group's "Sporting Secretary", W.W. Richards wrote that "this sight of nature's bounty, spread broadcast, might well gladden the hearts of millions of human beings in times to come, who, escaping from the clash and turmoil of a greater San Francisco, seek the enjoyment, the invigoration, the elevation and refinement of this glorious heritage handed down to us through the centuries". Richards, a wealthy sportsman, was also Secretary of the California Game and Fish Protective Association, a major supporter of the park plan envisioning Big Basin as a game preserve. "As each succeeding year diminishes the game supply and renders efficient laws for its protection the more necessary", Richards wrote in the *San Jose Mercury*, "we of the rod and gun see in the acquirement of this grand forest a magnificent home and refuge for our game and fish peculiar to the State." Richards, like other Sempervirens Club members, envisioned a greater park, eventually one of 60,000 acres, purchased with legislative aid and private subscriptions. It would be enthusiastically supported by "every one of the 20,000 sportsmen of our glorious State". He saw Big Basin as a "breeding refuge" for deer, pigeons, squirrels, quail, and other game desired by hunters in the adjacent counties. "For, lo, all good things of the earth were made by the Almighty for the proper use of man", Richards wrote, voicing a sentiment that would later come to be termed "anthropocentrism".

Louise Jones wrote that "into this sanctuary, the common thoughts and petty cares of daily life dare not intrude; here is peace, serene and perfect rest". A Quaker, Mrs. Jones had been a teacher of poor children in Arkansas and Hawaii. She had camped in Big Basin while teaching school in nearby Pescadero. As a journalist for national publications, she had reported on Rutherford B. Hayes' campaign for President. Louise Jones had lived in Germany with her husband, a classics scholar, before coming to San Jose where she became first President of the San Jose Woman's Club. She was also the mother of California State Senator Herbert Jones, who would himself play a pivotal role in the Sempervirens Club.

Clerics were involved in the preservation efforts as well. For the Rev. Edwin Sidney Williams, a retired Congregational minister from nearby Saratoga, "the chief reason for my growing interest in Sempervirens Park is its beneficial effect on the people of the State, particularly the working people of the bay cities". He added that what

Sempervirens Club founding member W.W. Richards.

*Photo: Andrew P. Hill, Sempervirens Fund Collection*

charmed him was the "true democracy" of the park:

*and in working for it, though the least of the workers, I am working for the better California. No street arab will go back from the grandeur and the beauty of these primeval forests untouched. The higher influences of American life will have a better chance at him if he senses what the State has done in appointing him one of the guardians of God's great trees. And the poor sewing girls can come at slight expense and need no other chaperon than the gracious matron in the park.*

Father Robert E. Kenna, Jesuit President of Santa Clara College and an influential participant in the Sempervirens Club activities, agreed that Big Basin should be a people's park for holiday outings, "a place whither our children and workmen, factory girls and others breathing all the week impure air, might, amidst the great trees and along rippling brooks, breathe pure air and rest amidst those great forests, where their minds and hearts are lifted to higher, purer, nobler things".

Indicative of a larger regional interest in the park, the first public meetings of the Sempervirens Club were held in July and August 1900, at the Palace Hotel in San Francisco. A significant decision was made to appeal to the California Legislature instead of the United States Congress for a park, in part to avoid jeopardizing the passage of another bill already pending to purchase the Calaveras Big Trees in the Sierra. An additional reason to seek state protection was the opposition by Eastern politicians to creating more federal parks in the west. Among Californians, there was also resistance to increased federal control of state territory. Certainly Congress was unwilling to purchase private property for forest preservation while so much federal land remained unoccupied. That same year, representatives from the Sempervirens Club attended the two political party conventions in California and successfully solicited the support of both parties for state action.

Although the focus was now solely on the Big Basin, interpreted as the Waddell watershed, many people wanted to link together all 35,000 acres of remaining old-growth redwoods in San Mateo as well as Santa Cruz counties. In their support, the *San Francisco Examiner* argued that there were "two reasons why this grove should

be preserved. One is that it is one of the finest tracts of the sequoia sempervirens, and is within easy reach of the centers of population; and in the second place, it is the source of a considerable part of the water supply of San Francisco, and of the towns of San Mateo and Santa Cruz Counties". Sempervirens Club President Charles Wesley Reed told the San Francisco Board of Supervisors that there were only forty-four square miles of standing timber left south of the city, and that they must act quickly. "The interest of San Francisco in the preservation of the trees lies in the fact that if they are destroyed a very important portion of San Francisco's water supply will be ruined." Reed further contended that the state money spent would "give us at the doors of San Francisco this wonderful forest as a heritage forever". The *San Jose Mercury*, commenting on a report in the *Stockton Independent* that the citizens of San Francisco themselves should purchase Big Basin, editorialized in June 1900, that state ownership would achieve the objectives of "conservation of the water supply, the maintenance of an equable temperature in the fertile and productive valleys of Santa Cruz, San Mateo and Santa Clara counties, and the saving intact of a forest of Sempervirens trees which are rapidly disappearing from California, and which grow nowhere else in the world".

The fear of climate change was an important motive for preventing the deforestation of the surrounding hills. In 1902, Carrie Stevens Walter would write in the *Overland Monthly* that "the cutting of these redwood forests has materially lessened the rainfall of the region". She added that in Boulder Creek, "the rainfall has decreased more than one half since its surrounding hills were denuded of their heavy forests". Agricultural interests in San Jose feared that more cutting of the redwoods in the Santa Cruz Mountains would turn the Santa Clara Valley into a desert. If the timber cutters have their way, predicted the *Santa Cruz Surf*, "in two years the region instead of possessing Edenic aspects, will be worse than a Sahara".

Beyond concerns for climatic change and water supply to nearby metropolitan areas, tourism was becoming a consideration in the preservation efforts. An editorial in the *Boulder Creek Mountain Echo* in December 1900, boasted that "the Big Basin project is making Boulder Creek quite famous throughout the state". From the beginning, local interests in this logging town, which would become the gateway to the park, were solidly in favor of preservation. Creation of the park would "draw the eyes of the state in this direction", the editorial continued. "Especially would it attract men of wealth to these mountains, which are already become famous as a place for the summer homes of our city cousins". Real estate and tourism were the obvious economic replacements for the logging industry which was facing its demise as the forests disappeared. By April 1901, the *Mountain Echo* would predict that:

*(I)f we rise to our opportunity that park may bring a hundred thousand dollars a year in revenue to this county...it will rise into worldwide fame, as one of the seven natural wonders of the modern world and be named in the list with the Yosemite Valley, the Yellowstone Park, Niagara Falls, the Mammoth Cave and the Natural Bridge of Virginia, and Santa Cruz may turn all this fame to her own pecuniary advantage if she so wills.*

After the 1900 fall election, Sempervirens Club President Charles Wesley Reed drafted a bill proposing the "California Redwood Park." On January 15, 1901, Assemblymember George H. Fisk of San Francisco introduced the proposal as Assembly Bill 200. The bill sought to create a commission to purchase a grove of *Sequoia sempervirens* in order "to preserve a body of these trees from destruction and maintain them for the honor of California and the benefit of succeeding generations". It set a maximum acquisition price of $500,000 to purchase 5,000 acres at $100 an acre — Middleton's asking price. It called for the immediate appropriation of half that sum. Speaking before hearings by the Committee on Public Lands and Forests were Sempervirens Club members Reed, Dudley and Father Kenna; and Mrs. E.O. Smith, founder of the San Jose Woman's Club. In February 1901, AB 200 was rejected by the Assembly Ways and Means Committee for fiscal reasons.

At an emergency meeting of the Sempervirens Club, Andrew Hill was appointed a committee of one to go to Sacramento with his photographs of Big Basin and its old-growth trees, as well as scenes of devastation from recent logging. He met with popular Assemblymember Alden Anderson, son of San Jose orchard farmer John Z. Anderson. The Assemblymember made some suggestions on how the proposal might be modified and advised Hill to seek the help of

Loggers proudly display their abilities.
*Photo: Covello and Covello Collection*

veteran Sacramento Assemblymember Grove L. Johnson, leader of the Southern Pacific Railroad Company's political machine and father of future Progressive Governor Hiram Johnson. The powerful legislator agreed to sponsor the revised bill which set the total appropriation to $250,000 for 2,500 acres and spread the purchase over five years. It specified "Big Basin" as the site of the purchase.

Hill decided to seek Catholic support for the bill since Catholic members of the legislature constituted a substantial minority and tended to vote together. Father Kenna, who had been Hill's roommate at Santa Clara Prepartory School, invited him to speak to a group of Jesuit priests visiting Big Basin. They agreed to spread the word to their parishes throughout the state and to urge support of the legislation.

Some Sempervirens Club members were not pleased with the reduction of the park to 2,500 acres. In a 1901 article in the *San Francisco Chronicle*, Carrie Stevens Walter had argued for a park of from 35,000 to 60,000 acres which would cost an estimated $2,500,000. "Imagine a time in the not very remote future when the whole peninsula from San Francisco to San Jose shall become one great city; then picture, at its very doorway, this magnificent domain of redwood forest and running streams, the

14

breathing place of millions of cramped and crowded denizens of the city. (This park) is a heritage of which we have no right to deprive future generations". She went on to suggest that scientific forestry, "according to the best German methods", and under the direction of the Bay Area's two great universities, would help pay for the care and "improvement" of the park. Writing in the April 1901 *Stanford Sequoia*, Professor Dudley was another who felt the park described by the revised bill, which he called an "urgency measure", was too small. "Since the beginning, it has been the plan of those who have given the matter the most attention to secure ultimately all or nearly all the land that lies between the Butano-Pescadero watershed on the north and Ben Lomond on the south. The tract thus outlined would include from 28,000 to 39,000 acres". Dudley argued that "for scientific purposes, and even for a good public park", at least 30,000 acres was needed. The amount to be appropriated, which would purchase only 2,500 acres, is a good start, but "valuable tracts must be acquired in other parts of the greater park, and finally the gaps closed and the park completed".

Another visitor to the redwoods was Delphin M. Delmas, San Francisco attorney and acclaimed orator who also owned a 300 acre vineyard in Mountain View. Delmas agreed to speak to the legislators on behalf of Johnson's bill, AB 873. He told the politicians, "You experience a feeling of profound sadness as you conjure up the picture of these venerable trees falling hacked and shivered, to become the common place materials of barter and trade. As you behold their lofty foliage stirred by the ocean breeze, you seem to hear them murmur a prayer to be saved from such desecration". According to Delmas, three objections had been raised by opponents of the park: that the trees ought to be given by the wealthy owners to the state rather than bought by taxpayers; that the price asked by them was too high, and that the state should pay only for necessities, not "mere taste and sentiment". Delmas argued that gifts cannot be forced from land owners, and that even if the land was donated it would not absolve the state from its responsibilities. As to value, Delmas asked, "Has the forest no value beyond the number of thousand feet of lumber in its trees". He continued:

*The states of Europe — France and Germany notably — lay out yearly vast sums in the preservation of such remnants of forests as are left them. New York and Massachusetts do the same. The city of San Francisco has expended millions to convert the sand-dunes of her suburbs into her Golden Gate Park...In the face of these examples shall California hesitate to spend the modest figure named in this bill to secure for all coming generations a park planted and nurtured by the never-tiring hand of Nature, compared with whose primeval grandeur man's work is but a paltry imitation?*

Finally, the orator called upon the politicians' religious sensibilities. "Man's work, if destroyed, man may again replace. God's work, God alone can re-create. Accede, then, to the prayers of the people. Save this forest. Save it now." By all accounts, his speech was a *tour de force*.

W.W. Richards and fishing party.
*Photo: Andrew P. Hill, Sempervirens Fund Collection*

15

Additional hurdles would remain, but Andrew P. Hill, was indefatigable. The property owners demanded a guarantee of $50,000 to extend the option on the land in case the state should fail to make its first payment on time. Father Kenna was able to obtain funds from his wealthy and powerful nephew, James Phelan, Mayor of San Francisco. Ironically this was at the same period that Phelan was filing a claim for a reservoir site in Hetch Hetchy within the boundaries of Yosemite to secure water for his city. To communicate the news to politicians in Sacramento that the option had been extended, Hill persuaded the editor of the *San Jose Mercury* to write an editorial in a special edition of the paper, and he took a pre-dawn train to the capital to personally deliver copies of the paper to all of the legislator's desks. The Assembly passed the California Redwood Park Bill by a vote of fifty-five to one. The bill then went to the Senate where it was introduced by Senator Charles M. Shortridge, attorney John E. Richards' law partner in San Jose. Speaking on its behalf in that chamber was Father Kenna, who told the Senators:

*I do not come to speak to you as a priest, nor as the president of a great college, nor in the language of such, but as a 'Forty-niner,' and in the language of one who loves the great land of the West, and her magnificent forests which so often charmed my boyhood days...these redwoods are pre-eminently Californian, unique in their species and situation, and as a "forty-niner" I beg you to stay the hand that would harm those that still remain to recall the glories of those vast virgin forests now no more.*

The bill passed the Senate almost unanimously.

Governor Henry T. Gage was then presented with two forestry measures for his signature. One was the park bill, and the other would create a forestry and irrigation commission to plan a comprehensive policy of forest and land protection. The latter had wide support, particularly from railroad and agricultural interests. In order to hold to his campaign promise of economy in government, Gage felt he could only sign one. Hill went into action again, sending telegrams to park partisans all over the state asking them to voice their immediate support. A public hearing was held by Governor Gage and the Sempervirens Club at which time Professor Dudley and other scientists from Stanford and the University of California at Berkeley spoke in favor of the park as an invaluable botanical garden in which Bay Area students would have the opportunity to study. Stanford's President Jordan, told the governor that the forestry and irrigation bill could wait while "any delay in connection with the proposed (park) might be fatal". Gage signed the park bill on March 16, 1901, announcing that now "poor and rich alike might enjoy the pleasures of these grand groves of nature".

When President Theodore Roosevelt visited California in 1903, he lauded the establishment of the park, saying that "the interest of California in forest protection was shown even more effectively by the purchase of the Big Basin Redwood Park, a superb forest property, the possession of which should be a source of just pride to all citizens jealous of California's good name".

The California Redwood Park Bill could only set plans for the park in motion. The land still had to be

Ox team on logging skid road, circa 1875.    *Photo: Covello and Covello Historical Collection*

Couple at Sempervirens Falls.
*Photo: Andrew P. Hill, Sempervirens Fund Collection*

purchased. Governor Gage appointed five members, including himself, to the Redwood Park Commission created by the legislation. Two Commissioners were academics: Father Kenna and Professor Dudley. Two were railroad men: Arthur W. Foster, President of the North Pacific Coast Railway and a Regent of the University of California; and William H. Mills, land agent for the Southern Pacific Railway Company. In addition to serving as Collis P. Huntington's right hand, Mills was the editor-publisher of the *Sacramento Record-Union* newspaper, and had been on state commissions debating the future of Yosemite and of Lake Tahoe. A supporter of irrigation for small farms, he had favored the water bill vetoed by the governor. He complained that the price of the park purchase at $100 an acre was too high — he thought $30 more appropriate — and that Big Basin was too remote. Eventually an Advisory Board convinced the Redwood Park Commission that the board-feet of standing timber was a great deal more than earlier estimated, making much of the land worth in excess of $100 an acre; and that recent sawmilling operations developed in the area had increased its accessibility. When the original option to purchase expired, the Sempervirens Club received an extension. When the extension ran out, Irvin T. Bloom, one of the property owners involved, grew tired of waiting and cut the redwoods on his 320

acres of the proposed park.

Redwood Park Commission meetings were emotional affairs, as disagreements exploded into shouting matches. Mills was frequently at odds with the other commissioners. However, he did agree with Dudley's vision of a "greater park", writing that he was in favor of "from 10 to 14,000 acres eventually. The State can afford to do this". Dudley was disenchanted with Sempervirens Club activists Charles Wesley Reed and W.W. Richards, calling them "mountebanks". He wrote to Father Kenna that "the Sempervirens people have apparently become a little crazy on this matter" when they pressured the Commission for a speedy decision on purchasing land. After Father Kenna resigned from the Commission, Dudley wrote him that "I have felt that only you looked at the park with feelings similar to my own".

Finally in September 1902, over a year and a half after passage of the legislation, the Commission signed documents purchasing 2,500 acres of prime redwood from Henry L. Middleton for $250,000. Middleton included 800 acres of chaparral and 500 acres of cut-over or burned land capable of reforestation in the deal. The California Redwood Park in Big Basin could soon open its 3,800 acres to the public.

Sempervirens Falls on Sempervirens Creek today.
*Photo: Alexander Lowry, Sempervirens Fund Collection*

17

Scenic Trail, Big Basin Redwoods State Park. *Photo: Alexander Lowry, Sempervirens Fund Collection*

# IV.

## Sempervirens Club and the New State Park

*The Sempervirens Club is one of the ideal clubs of the twentieth century, in that it comprises both men and women.*

**Club Life, February 1904**

With the land for a state park in Big Basin finally purchased, the *Boulder Creek Mountain Echo* would announce: "THE PARK IS OURS". But, as *Santa Cruz Surf* Editor Arthur Taylor pointed out, "the present area of the park is only a nucleus for what the park ought to embrace". The goal of a "greater park" remained for many club members. When Louise Jones wrote her memoirs for the *Journal of the International Society of Arboriculture* in 1903, she noted, "instead of dissolving, as a body whose work is finished, the club underwent a reorganization and had a larger membership than ever". In the future, the Sempervirens Club planned to "work for the acquisition of adjoining territory, for the enlarging and beautifying of the tract thus rescued from destruction".

The remaining Club activists Andrew Hill, Carrie Stevens Walter, Louise Jones, and W.W. Richards turned to San Franciscan Laura White for help in establishing the Club on a permanent footing. White had published short sketches in Bret Harte's *Overland Monthly* and had met Walter and Josephine Clifford McCrackin, who had also written for the literary monthly in the 1880's. Married to banker Lovell White who was an associate of Comstock Lode "King" William Ralston, Laura White had been active in the campaign for women's suffrage in 1896 along with Phoebe Hearst, Emma Shafter Howard and other notable Bay Area women. The year after the unsuccessful vote on women's suffrage, she founded the California Club to pursue a reform agenda. In the spring of 1900, she enlisted her fellow club members in the battle to save the giant Sequoias of Calaveras.

The campaign to preserve the Sierra sequoias had begun when a Wisconsin lumber baron purchased an option on 8,000 acres of land that included two groups of sequoias six miles apart, the Mammoth Grove in Calaveras County and the South Park Grove in Tuolumne County. San Franciscans learned of this development from Stanford President David Starr Jordan several months before he hosted the Big Basin meeting at Stanford. At a public meeting he described the Calaveras grove as "the noblest forest in the world", and said it was "more the duty of the nation to preserve its forests than to foster commerce". In the audience were members of the California Club who resolved to do what they could to stop the destruction. They wrote letters, contacted influential people, and mobilized a growing network of club women across the country.

Mrs. A.D. Sharon, California Club Vice President, was given the task of alerting federal legislators to the emergency. The first protests resulted in a joint Congressional resolution instructing the Secretary of the Interior to take steps to acquire the land. It was passed by Congress and signed by President McKinley on March 8, 1900. However, the rights of the owner to sell were upheld by the courts, and the lumberman took possession of the property in April. Officials were reluctant to acquire the property by condemnation. So while the federal government's acquisition of the Sierra Big Trees was stalled, Laura White turned her attention to their kin, the coastal redwoods.

After taking office as its president in January 1903, Laura White announced that the objectives of the reformed Sempervirens Club were "to promote the interests and development of the park in whatever manner may lie within the province of such an organization". She said that this included encouraging "the advancement of scientific forestry in California", and broadening the scope of conservation efforts "to assist when necessary in the preservation of other groves of Sequoia — both sempervirens and gigantea — and of other natural wonders with which our state is so lavishly endowed". To this end, White encouraged the formation of local chapters of the Sempervirens Club throughout the state and appointed well-known Vice Presidents-at-large, including John Muir, San Francisco Mayor James Phelan, Phoebe Hearst, Louise Jones, and former Lt. Governor William Jeter. The Ebell Club of Los Angeles joined as an affiliate; and one of its prominent members, Abbot Kinney, was appointed a Vice President of the Sempervirens Club. Kinney had visited Big Basin in 1887 with Ralph Sidney Smith, while a member of the State Board of Forestry. He was the developer who would be responsible for the establishment of a Southern California version of Venice complete with canals, and he actively sought Sempervirens Club support in reserving Griffith Park in the Los Angeles area as an experimental station for planting eucalyptus trees.

Branches of the Sempervirens Club were formed in San Francisco, San Jose, Alameda, Berkeley, Paso Robles, Los Gatos, and elsewhere. In Butte County, pioneer settler John Bidwell was President of the local branch of the Club. Typical of the local branches was Boulder Creek, where more than eighty people in the small community bordering Big Basin became members after paying the one dollar dues. W.S. Rodgers, one of the original Club supporters, reported in his *Boulder Creek Mountain Echo*, that "ladies are being solicited to join as well as the men and it is hoped to get many of them interested". Female assistance was vitally necessary in the proposed work of the Club, he wrote, "which is to assist in preserving, beautifying and enlarging the state park in the Big Basin and opening a good highway thereto". The Boulder Creek club's first President was Samuel Rambo, merchant and former State Senator who would become the new park's second Warden. When in April 1903, Father Kenna resigned from the Redwood Park Commission, the local Club was instrumental in convincing the Governor to appoint Santa Cruz tanner Henry Kron to replace him.

In January 1904, the Sempervirens Club held its annual convention at the Palace Hotel in San Francisco. In its glowing account of the meeting, *Club Life* magazine reported that the organization now had over 300 members with local branches all over the state. After success was achieved in saving the Big Basin redwoods, "the lust of power was upon the members then, and they sighed for more worlds to conquer", according to the publication. With its avowed purpose of forwarding the cause of scientific forestry in the state, the Sempervirens Club was "one of the ideal clubs of the twentieth century, in that it comprises both men and women" in its membership and among its officers, which at the time included East Bay publisher and legislator Joseph Knowland, and the wife of Berkeley scientist and Sierra Club geologist Joseph LeConte. At the annual meeting, resolutions were passed seeking "the enactment of laws providing for the State regulation of the harvesting of timber and the reforesting of denuded lands, and for more efficient protection of our forests from fires". The Club also supported the creation of more forest reserves in California by the federal government and the efforts of the Outdoor Art League, founded in Mill Valley in 1902 by Laura White, to secure the purchase of the Calaveras Big Trees.

The California Redwood Park officially opened to campers on June 1, 1904. A month later, the Sempervirens Club held its first encampment there. More than two dozen Club members spent several days in the Sempervirens Camp, and President White told the *Boulder Creek Mountain Echo*, "the club must make at least one pilgrimage a year to its innermost recesses as an appreciation of this most glorious achievement of the people of our State." The guest of honor was botanist Hugo De Vries from Holland. I.T. Bloom, who had impatiently logged his Big Basin redwoods when Redwood Park Commissioners were slow in purchasing land, had become a Club member and donated four and one-half acres for a club site adjacent to the park. Josephine Clifford McCrackin wrote that "next year, if fortune favors us, our annual reunion will be held in this House Beautiful...With the erection of this building and the completing of the Park Warden's Lodge, a new era in the Big Basin will begin".

One of the new park's camping areas became known as Governor's Camp, following a July 1904 visit of Governor George C. Pardee, who had succeeded Henry T. Gage. Redwood Park Commission members joined him to formally

## Santa Cruz Morning Sentinel

PUBLISHED BY

### Duncan McPherson & Chas. W. Waldron,
#### PROPRIETORS.

Office: Cor. Pacific Av. and Locust St.

RATES OF SUBSCRIPTION:

One year (entirely in advance)...$5 00

One year (if not in advance)......$6 00

One month (by mail or carrier)..50 cts

ADVERTISING RATES.

Legal and Political.

Square (nine lines or less) first insertion ...........................$1 50

Each subsequent insertion .......$1 00

## "WEEKLY SENTINEL."

RATES OF SUBSCRIPTION:

One year (if not in advance)......$2 00
One year (entirely in advance).... 1 50
One month (by mail or carrier).. 20 cts

THIS PAPER is kept on file at E. C.
DAKE'S Advertising Agen-
cy, 64 and 65 Merchants Exchange, San Francisco, California, where contracts for advertising can be made for it.

## COUNTY OFFICIAL PAPER.

### DUNCAN McPHERSON, EDITOR.

THIS MORNING'S EDITION,     1,930

### TRIP INTO THE BIG BASIN.

This is a delightful part of the year for a trip into the Big Basin. Of course the road from Boulder Creek, where not watered, is dusty, but it is well watered for a large part of the distance up the mountain, and the trails through the Big Basin are now so numerous and free from fallen timber that this incomparable body of tree giants is no longer an unknown country.

Two good wagon roads reach the margin of the forest, in fact penetrate it for a short distance, enabling the visitor to drive within two miles of Camp Gage, where pedestrianism or horseback riding is resorted to. One of these roads is known as the Big Basin Co. road and the other as the Bloom grade. The writer went in over the first and came out over the second, the return trip, twenty-two miles, partly on foot, partly on horseback, and for twenty miles, from the top of the mountain, behind a lively team, in three hours and twenty minutes from Camp Gage to Santa Cruz.

For several weeks the date of the visit to the Big Basin Park by the Big Basin Commission, with Gov. Gage at the head, has been an uncertainty, but it was finally brought about last week, and Friday evening a "Sentinel" representative arrived at Boulder Creek on his way to what is to be the great Forest Play Ground of California. As early as three o'clock the next morning he heard jingling bells, and looking into the night he saw long teams carrying lanterns and moving in the direction of the mountains. They were to return with split timber or lumber obtained at the Little Basin saw-mill, located some distance south of Big Basin.

At 5:30 the "Sentinel" reporter was roused from his slumber, to be on the road after a hurried breakfast. The road was up and up to the summit, and then down to the "Rocks," or what is now known as Camp Hill, the time consumed being an hour and a half in making the trip. This was the west end of wagon navigation. Here was met H. L. Middleton and saddled horses. A ride down the basin of two and a half miles, on an easy grade and through an unbroken forest of as handsome trees, redwood, spruce pine, chestnut oak, madrone, etc., as eyes ever gazed on, brought us to Camp Gage, where we found Gov. Henry T. Gage, Wm. H. Mills, General Chipman, A. W. Foster, Prof. W. R. Dudley, Father Kenna, all Park Commissioners, and Henry Lindlay and Drury Malone, advisors of the Commission, and artist A. P. Hill of San Jose and J. F. Coope, members of the Sempervirens Club and representing the counties of Santa Clara and Santa Cruz.

The day was spent in making trips of exploration in different directions, one of them being down the Basin to the lower proposed line, near the gorge on Waddell Creek, east branch.

Rain commenced falling in the early evening, but Manager Middleton had made such perfect and full arrangements for the entertainment of his guests, that all said, as they say in Spain: "Let it rain". A comfortable cook house and dining room, and a building for bed rooms, had been erected of lumber packed in on horses. Beyond this were a number of tents, supplied with good beds and toilet conveniences, each person having a tent or room for himself. The table was supplied with the best of food, wine and cigars, and two waiters to serve them. The evening was advantageously spent in studying the map of the 2,500 acres of land it is proposed to convert into a park. The forenoon of the next day was spent in riding three miles up and down hills, over ridges, to the west branch of the Waddell Creek, and the trip was through a continuous forest of redwood trees, with the exception of a small opening, say 200x300 feet. These trees, standing on the very tops of the ridges, were a pleasant surprise to the Commissioners who had not previously been over the ground. They had overlooked the fact that these ridges were a part of the Basin, and much lower than the rim of the Basin, and to find them covered with saw-log timber pleased them much. Besides, the quantity of water flowing through the Basin in the dryest month of the year, also pleased them.

Not one word of disappointment, but many words of satisfaction were expressed by the Governor and his associate Commissioners, the timber experts in the party reserving their opinions till their conclusions are embodied in a report that this week is to be submitted to the Commission.

Just before going out of the Park Governor Gage said to the writer that he had no cause to regret his signature to the bill which appropriates $250,000 for the purchase of the Big Basin, the same to be dedicated to a State Park, and our private opinion, publicly expressed, is, that the Commissioners are all emphatically in favor of the measure, and delighted with the Big Basin, but as to what value they will place on the bonded land we have no opinion to express. Some of them spoke of the State securing more than the land bonded, and as these lands are owned by men who desire to sell them the friends of the Park have nothing to fear from this direction.

A great many people think a newspaper should have about a page of local news, whether anything happens or not. Deluded mortals! Local editors can not make people break their necks, commit suicide or do any of the other exciting things that go to make up the material out of which the local reporter delights to weave paragraphs. Furnishing domestic news when there is none is very much like extracting blood from a turnip. It is no more than fair that those who grumble at the lack of local news in their paper should stop and think whether they could not give the editor an item or two worth printing, and, if so, let them hold their peace or growl at their own remissness.

A short time since the cow was sad, she scarce could raise her head, begad! Her hoofs were sore, her tail was limp; her mane and bangs had lost their crimp. And miles she

---

This account of Governor Gage's visit to Big Basin was written by Duncan McPherson, editor of the *Santa Cruz Morning Sentinel*. It ran in the September 24, 1901 edition, the day it switched from a weekly to a daily newspaper.

*Courtesy of Mrs. Lillian McPherson Rouse, Granddaughter of Duncan, Private Collection*

take possession of the 3,800 acres purchased by the state. Santa Cruz County Horticultural Commissioner J.H.B. "Humphrey" Pilkington was appointed the first "Guardian" of the park. During his several weeks residence at the park, Governor Pardee was visited by Governor Heber Wells of Utah, California Congressman J.C. Needham, and the twenty-one member "Raisin City Band" of Fresno.

In August 1904, a major gathering of state officials and businessmen was hosted in the park by the State Board of Trade. More than 130 people attended and the event featured a barbecue, serving "bulls-head, beef and mutton; roasted clams" and other delicacies, and entertainment by a full orchestra. Several speakers referred to the campaign for recession of Yosemite to the national government and their hopes that the $25,000 annual appropriation in state money would be transferred from Yosemite to Big Basin. Among the resolutions passed by the guests was one strongly urging "the enlargement of the forest boundaries by the purchase of bordering tracts, some of which have been lumbered, but will be rapidly reforested if protected from fire", in the belief that "such enlargement of the park (is) necessary to its protection and proper administration". In November, the Commission would change Pilkington's title to "Park Warden" and the name of the park would officially be designated "California Redwood Park".

But in September 1904, before those changes could be completed, the fortunes of the new park would be drastically diminished when a fire started in a sawdust pile at a new mill north of the park. During the next twenty days, flames raced through the redwoods to the sea, burning 1,200 acres. While the center area of the park was protected by the heroic efforts of Pilkington and his crew of one hundred men, the effects of the fire on the environment of the new park were disastrous. The *Mountain Echo* bemoaned, "The beautiful trees of the Big Basin, saved from the woodman's axe only by the devoted efforts of a society of nature lovers, have been seared by the flames, and many of them destroyed". Some of the scars can still be seen in the park today.

From the establishment of the park, access into it had been an urgent topic of conversation among Sempervirens Club members as well as among everyone interested in how tourism might benefit those communities in its path. For over a decade, ideas were proposed and politicians in the three counties surrounding the park and in Sacramento argued over who would pay for the proposed highways or roads. The *Santa Cruz Sentinel* reported that local capitalist and Club member Frederick A. Hihn and a County Supervisor were interested in a road up Waddell Creek to the park from the coast. "The city of Santa Cruz, and the county at large, are interested in having the Big Basin penetrated from both sides", said Hihn in August 1903. The plan for a coast road competed with Andrew Hill's idea that a road from Santa Clara County should be constructed into the Santa Cruz Mountains alongside Stevens Creek. Sempervirens Club members in San Jose, where the organization had its greatest strength, began to lobby strongly for a road to the park from the east. Besides improving the old road from the train station in Boulder Creek to the park, road work was also needed to connect existing camp sites, including Sempervirens Camp next to Slippery Rock where the Club was started, to others within the park boundaries.

In the fall of 1904, Santa Cruz County Supervisors allocated $12,000 for a more direct route into the park via Boulder Creek, awarding the construction contract to the Granite Rock Company of Watsonville. In San Jose, members of the local Sempervirens Club, led by district attorney James H. Campbell, petitioned the state for a similar amount to finance construction of a road into the park via the Saratoga Gap. The committee to investigate this proposal included Andrew Hill and Saratoga minister Edwin S. Williams. Bills were introduced in the State Senate and Assembly for the Saratoga road but the Governor said he was unwilling to finance anything other than maintenance inside the park.

In order to accept the land donated by I.T. Bloom for a Club site, it was determined that the Sempervirens Club would have to incorporate, which would not be completed until 1907. Andrew Hill and Civil Engineer A.T. Hermann, whose wife had been among the first members of the Club, surveyed land on the border of Big Basin on which to build summer homes. And Club supporter John E. Richards, soon to be Judge Richards, said that he would build a country home adjoining the clubhouse site.

The primary goal of the Sempervirens Club seemed to have been achieved. Some of the founding members had considered disbanding the club. Several turned to other pursuits. Charles Wesley Reed took up railroad construction and with mule teams built considerable portions of the Ocean Shore, Northern Electric, Western Pacific, Sacramento Southern Railways, as well as the Harriman lines in Mexico and the Imperial Valley. In the Hiram Johnson administration, Reed conducted the prosecution of corruption, incompetence, and mismanagement uncovered in state institutions and served as President of the first California Civil Service Commission. He retired on a ranch near Chico and tended his orchard. J.F. Coope was in his early forties when he died of diphtheria. An elderly John Q. Packard died from heart failure in 1908. Roley Kooser entered the plumbing business in San Jose and later became secretary of the Home Owners Building and Loan Association.

At the Club's annual meeting in January 1906, Laura White declined re-election and her place was taken by the Reverend Eli McClish, President of the College of the Pacific, then located in San Jose. In her final report to the Sempervirens Club membership, Mrs. White spoke of San Jose as "the camping ground of the original band of stalwarts, who through pluck and determination acquired the park". She said that "to reorganize a Club whose fire of enthusiasm has already been spent in the pursuit and attainment of its early object is not the easy task which it is supposed to be by some". Since the park and "all the forestry interests of California are now in competent hands...already scientific methods are introduced in the Government Reserves and that trees are being cut and sold in limited numbers", White said the club need no longer worry about the park but should devote its efforts to the proposed Saratoga road, in addition to the "bijou park" to be built for members on I.T. Bloom's land, and on behalf of the purchase of the Calaveras groves of big trees.

McClish's tenure with the Club was to be short. After April 1906, he became distracted by what the *Boulder Creek Mountain Echo* termed "the recent earthquake confusion" which devastated San Francisco and damaged many of the buildings on the University of the Pacific campus. Disturbance in the park was slight and in May, the new road, constructed under contract by Bloom and passing through a portion of his property,

**Park Commissioners and Advisory Board visiting Big Basin, September, 1901**
(Left to Right) General Chipman, J.F. Coope, Prof. W.R. Dudley, William H. Mills, Henry Lindley, Father Kenna,
Gov. Henry T. Gage, John Green, D.M. McPherson.   *Photo: California State Park Collection*

23

was opened to the public. E.T. Allen resigned as State Forester and was replaced by another Pinchot nominee, G.B. Lull. Bids were taken for a telephone line into the park and operation of the Sempervirens Camp was taken over by Joseph Grahamer. "The big floor and other conveniences fixed up by the club are still there", reported the *Boulder Creek Mountain Echo*, "and the grounds are to be made suitable for picnicking".

Reverend McClish resigned his post after the year was up to accept a preaching ministry in Los Angeles. He was replaced as Club President by Kate Moody Kennedy, a leader in the San Jose Woman's Club along with Carrie Stevens Walter and Louise Jones, the wife of a prominent San Jose attorney. Kate Moody Kennedy, like Carrie Stevens Walter and Judge John Richards, was a leading light in the literary community of San Jose and a friend of poets Edwin Markham and Ina Coolbrith, the state's first Poet Laureate. Under her leadership, the Sempervirens Club of California was incorporated on March 16, 1907, for the purposes of "the improvement and development of the State Sempervirens Forest to the use and for the benefit of the people of California, and to encourage the preservation from destruction of other groves of Sequoia sempervirens and Sequoia gigantea, as well as other wooded groves, and to actively aid in immuning them from fires and to promote the general interests of scientific forestry in the State of California". In addition, the Club looked to its future form by declaring its desire "to acquire by gift, grant, devise or otherwise, lands and real estate, and to improve, mortgage, lease, sell or otherwise dispose of the same in the State of California". Besides President Kennedy, directors of the newly-incorporated Club included Andrew Hill and W.W. Richards; past Club Presidents White and McClish; Alexander Murgotten, editor of the *California Pioneer* and *California Elk*; San Jose Assessor Lewis Spitzer; William P. Lyon, business manager of the *Mercury*; soon-to-be U.S. Congressmember Arthur Free and his law partner William H. Rogers; and Mrs. A.T. Hermann, secretary of the Pratt Home for the elderly in San Jose. The once-indefatigable Carrie Stevens Walter was not able to serve due to illness and would die shortly after.

Established by the original park bill, the Redwood Park Commission was disbanded in 1905 by Governor Pardee. The Governor sided with Gifford Pinchot and the newly-established U.S. Forest Service in asserting forest "conservation", or efficient use of timber resources, rather than park "preservation" for any use other than scientific study or recreation. The result was legislation giving the Board of Forestry responsibility for the California Redwood Park. The Forestry Protection Act of 1905 abolished the already disbanded Redwood Park Commission and put the State Forester in charge of Big Basin. This effectively removed the park's protection from citizen oversight and put it solely in the hands of politicians. E.T. Allen, the State Forester recommended by Pinchot, was now in charge of the California Redwood Park at Big Basin.

The faith placed in state forestry protection by the Sempervirens Club was soon to be tested. In November 1906, Pilkington had been replaced as Park Warden by Samuel Rambo, a 65-year-old Boulder Creek merchant, former State Senator, and president of the Boulder Creek Sempervirens Club branch. Not long after Rambo took over, it was rumored that logging had resumed in the park. Both Rambo and State Forester G.B. Lull denied the allegations, saying that only dead or downed timber was being removed. Finally in February 1908, Sempervirens Club members investigated on their own and discovered, as Hill described, "this terrible devastation of the people's forest; this awful slaughter of live, beautiful trees". He reported seeing freshly-cut "wood, wood, wood everywhere. Pickets and posts and split timber over acres of ground as far as the eye could see." Much of the wood was from living, green redwood trees. The news was widely publicized in the press as "the rape of the redwoods". The group's report and Hill's photographs led to a Santa Cruz Grand Jury investigation, which temporarily put an end to logging in the park. Former Park Commissioner William Dudley wrote that "this incident of the legalized but wholly objectionable lumbering in the Park shows the people of this peninsula that the price of its most attractive natural feature is eternal vigilance, and not simply the $250,000 that was paid over from their state treasury".

In March 1908, the State Board of Forestry met in Palo Alto. Testifying before it were former Park Commissioners Dudley and Kenna, lumberman H.L. Middleton, and Judge Richards and Andrew Hill from the Sempervirens Club. While Park Warden Rambo, State Forester Lull and Lull's local representative, Deputy Warden

Creed, were not punished after the inquiry, the scandal reverberated in Sacramento and spawned no less than five bills calling for reorganization of the Board of Forestry. Lull angrily referred to members of the Sempervirens Club as "sickly sentimental women, and men with less sense than the women", and held on to his job through support from Governor Gillett, who proved to be no friend of conservation. Although it was well known that fire rarely killed these hardy trees, Lull's decision to cut and remove burned redwoods in Big Basin was backed by the Board of Forestry. It was also widely viewed as evidence for returning the park to civilian control. Two of the bills to revise the Forestry Act introduced in the 1909 legislative session were authored by Sempervirens Club members: Senator James B. Holohan of Watsonville and Assemblyman J.B. Maher of Santa Cruz. Both called for presidents or faculty members of the University of California, Stanford and Santa Clara College to serve four-year terms on the Board and neither mentioned the forester's responsibility for state parks. Maher's bill was amended to reinstate the old Redwood Park Commission. Members of the Club spoke before a joint committee of the California Senate and Assembly to investigate the cutting of live redwoods in the park, and a delegation from Sacramento visited the park along with Club officials. The *Boulder Creek Mountain Echo* expressed the hope that "no State Forester will ever again be allowed to attempt scientific forestry or exploit biological theories, so long as this shall remain a peoples' park". Although Maher's amended bill passed both houses, it was vetoed by Governor Gillette.

In 1910, Lull, who was never held accountable for his actions in Big Basin, resigned to work for an eastern company promoting the eucalyptus industry in California. At that time the *San Francisco Chronicle* recounted that "(a)bout a year ago Lull was under fire from the Sempervirens Club for ordering the destruction of the burned redwood trees in Big Basin, Santa Cruz County, but he maintained his place despite the influences against him". His successor as State Forester was George H. Homans who had trained at the

Biltmore Forest School, and who, according to one source, "was at his best before intellectual or social groups where he could expound in a scholarly manner upon the current needs of state forestry". Shortly after Hiram Johnson took over as Governor in 1911, Senator Holohan introduced a bill identical to the one Gillette vetoed two years before. It was passed quickly and Governor Johnson signed it on February 6, before reinstating the Redwood Park Commission. As commissioners to the reinstated Redwood Park Commission the Governor named *Santa Cruz Surf* editor Arthur Taylor; lumberman Henry Middleton; Father Robert Kenna from Santa Clara College; and Charles Wing, a professor of structural engineering at Stanford University who had mapped Big Basin with botanist William Dudley in the 1880's and who was at that time the Mayor of Palo Alto. William "Billy" Dool, a butcher, one-time Mayor of Boulder Creek, and friend of H.L. Middleton, was appointed the third Park Warden of California Redwood Park replacing Samuel Rambo. Dool was also appointed postmaster of the park. Dool's connection to the Sempervirens Club was apparent. When Phoebe Hearst donated $500 to Warden Dool for park projects, it was rumored the money was used to pay laborers to remove poison oak from camping areas. The *Boulder Creek Mountain Echo* editorialized that "our present park commissioners, Mrs. Hearst and Mr. Dool are all members of the Sempervirens Club of California, and thus it continues that all the best things for the park come to it through this club or its members. Also, *per contra*, it is some satisfaction that the late despoilers of the park were NOT members of this club". Editor Rodgers apparently forgot that Sam Rambo had been the founding President of the Club's Boulder Creek branch.

In 1908, Andrew Hill, acknowledged as the "savior of the redwoods" by so many of his contemporaries, was elected President of Sempervirens Club and would remain in that post for the next fourteen years.

Andrew P. Hill, the originator of the California Redwood Park, at the Father Tree.

*Photo: Hill Studio, Sempervirens Fund Collection*

# V.

## Toward the Vision of a "Greater Park"

*(The creation of a state park should only be upon land) abutting and contiguous, so that when the park was established it should be a continuous solid body... (purchasing entire) hydrographic districts.*

**William H. Mills, California Redwood Park Commissioner, 1902**

*I have a new scheme for buying the remaining lands within the basic rim that I think will succeed.*

**Andrew Hill, 1921**

Artist and photographer Andrew Putnam Hill spent almost a quarter of a century as the driving force behind the Sempervirens Club of California. His photographs of Big Basin redwood trees in their prime, as well as his scenes of the devastation wrought by logging, played a major role in convincing legislators that these trees should be protected and preserved in California's first state park.

From 1908 until his death in 1922, he served the Club as its president. For much of that time, he had a studio in Big Basin where he took and developed photographs, and led visitors on nature walks. During Hill's tenure, the Club successfully sought to remove the park from the control of the Board of Forestry which they blamed for "the rape of the redwoods" scandal. Through their efforts, a new highway was completed into the park from Santa Clara County in time for the opening of the Panama Pacific International Exposition in 1915. The Club finally secured title to public land in the Waddell Creek watershed from the federal government, nearly doubling the size of California Redwood Park.

The road that Andrew Hill had earlier envisioned from Santa Clara County did take a long time to achieve. By 1906, Hill had collected $800 from friends to pay for a survey of the proposed route by J.G. McMillan of Santa Clara County, but the San Francisco earthquake put a hold on any plans for roads

Andrew Hill's photo lab and studio in Big Basin.

*Photo: History San Jose Collection*

into the park from the coast or from San Jose. Business interests on the Santa Cruz side of the mountains could see little need for a road that bypassed their towns. In 1909, the *Boulder Creek Mountain Echo* declared itself "absolutely opposed" to a bill sponsored by the Sempervirens Club to appropriate $25,000 to build a road from Saratoga, saying it was unnecessary and impractical. Looking forward to the international exposition planned for San Francisco in 1915, Father Kenna wrote to Hill that it was:

*a crying shame that this great primeval park of the state has for ten years been practically ignored so far as real development and opening it to the public is concerned. The little that has been done...has not been in any way real work for the development of the Park for the whole people, which we want, and must have, (and) is possible, by 1915, when, we trust, we shall have good roads into the park, and a magnificent boulevard through it, so that the people of the old world, coming over by the million, may be shown over a grand state highway through this primeval redwood park.*

Hill sent out many circular letters over the next several years to Club members and supporters asking for their personal and financial assistance in obtaining the Saratoga road. In 1910 he wrote:

*When this road is built, the Park may be reached in less than four hours' ride from the leading hotels in San Francisco, the route traversing a country of great beauty and fertility, gradually rising from the Santa Clara Valley to the summit of the Santa Cruz Mountains at the Saratoga Gap. From this point one can see into eight counties of Central California. The length of the new state road outside of the Park will be about eleven miles from the summit to the rim of the Big Basin.*

According to editorial praise in the *San Jose Post*, Hill was "one of the greatest promotion agents in all California". He felt that "(w)e must exploit the sentiment of the great size and remote age of the forest and the trees" and "advertise the artistic beauty and botanical significance of its plant life and flora". Hill believed that these efforts would attract hundreds of thousands of people to the area and that the "valleys near San Francisco will settle up, and general prosperity will follow the opening of the Park". In a letter to Governor Johnson arguing for the Saratoga route, Andrew Hill wrote:

*Large automobile trucks will be ready to take sight seers into the Park, over this road, just as soon as it is completed and there is no doubt in my mind but that the Southern Pacific will build their line in very soon, thus creating more taxable property. We shall move for the construction of a large hotel somewhere within the Basin as soon as we are through with this Bill and all efforts of the Club shall be bent toward the development of the country along the line so as to create an increase in the values of property that the State may receive a good income on its investment.*

This booster mentality drew fire from Taylor of the *Santa Cruz Surf* who in an editorial accused Hill of wanting to open the park to recreation and the enhancement of private property, and said Hill was masquerading as a "friend of the forest".

At a meeting of the State Park Road Committee of the Sempervirens Club in December 1912, a resolution was passed to petition the State Highway Commission to construct a twelve-mile road into the park at a probable cost of $40,000. At the Club's annual dinner the following April, Hill reported that "the work of the Club for the coming year will be for the opening of an automobile and carriage road to the California Redwood Park for 1915, by the most direct route". According to Hill, a survey with maps and estimates had been done but "three times we have secured an appropriation by the legislature, for the new road, which unfortunately has each time been vetoed by the Governor". Hill sent out more urgent pleas for support and in August traveled to Sacramento with nine bound volumes of petitions signed by 43,000 people. Park Commission members Wing and Reverend James P. Morrisey, who had been appointed as the representative for Santa Clara College after Father Kenna's death, both supported the plan. By November, Hill was speaking to supervisors from the three adjoining counties about a $250,000 road program which would include the twenty-mile circular boulevard within the park that had been Father Kenna's dream. San Francisco civil engineer John E. Pope had surveyed the park and drawn up a map for the project that identified hills renamed after Father Kenna and Professor Dudley. That same month, Commissioner Wing traveled to Sacramento and spoke in favor of a $60,000 road from Saratoga.

Herbert Jones, the son of founding Sempervirens Club member Louise Jones, had

Senator Herbert Jones, Sempervirens Club
President from 1945 - 1968.

*Photo: Sempervirens Fund Collection*

grown up participating in Club activities. He had
earned a law degree from Stanford University
and was an attorney in San Jose when he
became the Club's secretary. In 1912, with strong
support from the Sempervirens Club, he was
elected to the State Senate. Writing to former
President Laura White, Hill bragged that "we
have succeeded in electing as Senator, Herbert
C. Jones...This will give us a speaker on the
floor of the Senate which should make us very
strong before the legislature". Soon after taking
office, Jones along with Senator William Flint
of San Benito County, introduced a bill that
according to Hill in his letter to the Governor
had been "practically drafted" by Professor
Charles Wing of Stanford, and which would
provide $100,000 "for survey and construction
of a state highway from Saratoga Gap...to, into
and within California Redwood Park in Santa
Cruz County". Hill took a delegation to the
Assembly Ways and Means Committee hearing
and, although the appropriation was cut to
$70,000, the bill was passed by both houses and
signed by Governor Johnson in June. The only
potential road block was a provision that right-
of-way had to be secured. Hill went into action
quickly and appealed to big donors for

contributions of up to $500 to purchase a 200
foot right-of-way over land containing virgin
redwoods owned by the Henry Cowell Estate.
He reached his necessary goal of $7602 with the
help of such wealthy Californians as James L.
Flood, James D. Phelan, Henry L. Tevis, A.B.
Spreckels, W.H. Crocker, Timothy Hopkins,
and W.H. Cowell. The *Mountain Echo* referred to
the right-of-way as "a sort of panhandle" to the
park; and it was over this land, many years
later, that the Sempervirens Fund would
construct the "Skyline-to-the-Sea Trail" between
Castle Rock and Big Basin Redwood State Parks.

Although there had been proposals to build a
road into Big Basin from the coast — the earliest
by local capitalist F.A. Hihn — they never met
with the same success as the proposal for a road
from Saratoga. In 1915, a bill to appropriate
$10,000 for a state highway from Pescadero to
the California Redwood Park did pass, and
Senator Flint announced that this "will make a
continuous highway from San Francisco through
Santa Cruz to Monterey and will be popular
with automobilists and give easy access to
mountains and sea beach". The bill died on the
Governor's desk. Money for the coast road was
not approved until 1927, and then only when
Senator Jones was willing to change its
description in the bill to a "fire escape road".

Another challenge which occupied Hill during
his long tenure as President of the Sempervirens
Club was the expansion of the boundaries of the
park. Many park supporters — among them
William Dudley and Carrie Stevens Walter —
envisioned a "greater park" of up to 60,000 acres

Governor Henry T. Gage at Big Basin 1904.

*Photo: History San Jose Collection*

in the Santa Cruz Mountains, and looked upon the original purchase of 3,800 acres as a necessary compromise to establish the park. Small additions were made by gifts from supporters of the park. I.T. Bloom donated four and one-half acres to the Sempervirens Club for a clubhouse, and Henry Middleton gave five acres to the state on which to construct the warden's lodge. The park boundary was increased further in 1917 and 1920, through donations totaling 200 acres from Judge Isaiah Hartman of Boulder Creek, a long-time Club member. From the beginning though, the Club had set its sights on unclaimed federal land in the Big Basin.

In 1906, Governor Pardee petitioned the federal government to cede nearly 3,000 acres in the chalk hills to the State of California for the park at Big Basin. About the same time, Senator George Perkins introduced a bill in Congress to donate all federal land between the park and the coast — about 3,250 acres with 840 acres in one tract — for the park. Apparently neither measure was successful. In 1911, as part of his bill that restored the Redwood Park Commission, State Senator Holohan included a resolution asking the federal government to cede lands to the park in Santa Cruz and San Mateo counties.

The following year, Representative Everis A. Hayes introduced another bill in Congress for the ceding of 4,000 acres of cut-over land called "The Chalks", to the State for the park. Congressmember Hayes was a long-time Sempervirens Club supporter along with his brother Jay with whom he also shared ownership of the *San Jose Mercury* newspaper. Hayes' bill was approved by the House Committee on Public Lands but apparently got no farther. The Sempervirens Club sent a "memorial" to Congress regarding the extension of the park towards the coast and fliers were sent to Congressional members on the issue. Senator Perkins reported that the bill had passed the Senate in June and "the park is now assured of an increase in area". Still nothing materialized.

In early 1913, Hill wrote to Secretary of the Interior Richard Ballinger for information about unlisted federal property. Hill said that the Sempervirens Club was "taking steps to acquire all the vacant lands between these detached parcels, owned by private parties, that the Park may become one great playground for the people of California and the world". Hill was told that some 3,440 acres had indeed been set aside for the park, but it was not until 1916 that title to land totaling 3,785 acres was transferred to California for the park. The property consisted of numerous small parcels, some of which continue to remain outside the watershed boundaries of Big Basin Redwoods State Park.

The road into the park over Saratoga summit was finally finished in May 1915, just in time to serve visitors to the Panama Pacific International Exposition in San Francisco. The Exposition celebrated the completion of the Panama Canal, as well as the market possibilities of Pacific Rim trade and the West Coast's superabundance of resources and beauty.

While real estate sales and developments contributed greatly to the influx of tourists into Boulder Creek in 1915, the prime drawing card to the area was the California Redwood Park in Big Basin. On May 18, 1915, at the Panama Pacific International Exposition, the Sempervirens Club began its celebration of the opening of the new road with a parade of members from the entrance of the grounds to the California Building. Before a large audience, Andrew Hill retold the history of how a dedicated band of preservationists had saved a remnant of redwoods in Big Basin which could now be seen not only by Californians but by visitors from around the world. "The Sempervirens Club of California is simply a name under which the people en masse have come together to organize and systematize the work of saving the big trees of California Redwood Park in order that it might be the most effective for the public good". In her address on "The Help of the Women of California in Acquiring the Park", former Club President Laura White acknowledged Josephine McCrackin for her role in initiating the preservation campaign, saying that "the initial step for the acquisition of this unparalleled piece of woods was taken by a woman" when her article, "SAVE THE TREES", was published in the *Santa Cruz Sentinel* on March 7, 1900. Also speaking at the event were Professor Charles Wing of Stanford, who described the long campaign for the Saratoga road; U.S. Senator James Phelan who praised the value of the park for education and civic bodies; State Senator William Flint, speaking on the park and the Legislature; Boulder Creek Judge Isaiah Hartman, who talked about mountain homes in the redwood district; and William Alexander, who discussed the value of the park to the business world. Exposition director P.T. Clay presented the Club with a bronze medal which was accepted by State Senator Herbert Jones.

Although the property given to them by I.T. Bloom remained undeveloped, Club members continued to hold an annual outing in Big Basin during the years Hill led them. At the 1908 Admissions Day gathering, event speakers included California Secretary of State Curry who said, "I don't want anything done in this park except to protect it and keep it as near as possible in a state of nature". Also speaking were Hill; Murgotten; Arthur Briggs of the State Board of Trade; Judge Richards; Professor Bell of Santa Clara; W.S. Rodgers, Editor of the *Boulder Creek Mountain Echo*; and Professor Johnson of Boulder Creek. In 1912, over one hundred Sierra Club members also camped in the park. At the Sempervirens Club outing in August of 1913, a banquet was held at which Hill, McCrackin, Father Kenna and Dudley were honored by assembled Club members. Another banquet was held in 1920, during

Andrew P. Hill, self portrait.
*Photo: Sempervirens Fund Collection*

which Club directors intended to "take up the subject of acquiring all of the lands within the rim of the Basin as promised by the Native Sons and other organizations of our state in the Park last summer". The original vision of a "greater park" was never far from President Hill's mind. As late as 1921, he wrote to Judge Hartman that "I have a new scheme for buying the remaining lands within the Basin rim that I think will succeed".

In a circular in May 1917, Hill alerted Club members to "a new danger that immediately threatens the park" and asked them to write their legislators urging them to support a Senate bill introduced by Jones to allocate $150,000 for more park land. According to Hill, land owners in the vicinity of the park were about "to erect a saw mill and cut off the timber, involving a serious hazard by fire, to the redwood forest and game preserve already in possession of the State...This timber must be obtained now or never". The funds requested by Jones were eventually made available in 1920 to purchase 800 acres from the Southern Lumber Company and 480 acres from the Western Shore Lumber Company. By the mid-1920's, the California Redwood Park had tripled in size to over 9,300 acres.

In 1919, several members of the Club formed the Forest Play Association in order to present a pageant in the park. "The Soul of Sequoia: A Forest Play", was written by Don Richards, a San Jose attorney and son of long-time Club member, Judge John E. Richards. The music was written by Thomas Cator, a well-known supporter of suffragette and anarchist causes in California, who had retired from political activism to become a composer in Carmel. The foreword in the play's program explained the plot: "From her long sleep Wawona comes with Sequoia, her brave lover, her voice thrills through the forest but dies away in sadness o'er Sequoia's slain body. The Padres, intoning the Misericordia, enter in time to save the Indian Maid from self-inflicted death. And last, Brundel, the woodsman, meets his master, the destroying ax is broken and the forest is preserved for ages yet unborn". Over 5,000 people saw the production when it was presented in September 1919, at the foot of a giant redwood in a natural amphitheater. It featured dancers and singers in Greek attire and players named "Soul of Man" and "Spirit of Nature". One review reported that, "(a)mong the leading actors was one of the

The "Soul of Sequoia: A Forest Play" players, September 1919.    *Photo: Sempervirens Fund Collection*

mountain deer, which, lured by the calls of the assistant park warden, had been tamed sufficiently for the appearance in the play". Herbert Jones remembered an incident "amusing in retrospect but serious at the time" after the performance when "hundreds of the audience were sleeping in their blankets in the open, with no protection against the weather. At about three or four o'clock in the morning, an unexpected downpour of rain produced great commotion as people hastily climbed into their cars or rushed for the protection of the dining room of the Inn".

The following year another production was mounted by Sempervirens Club members. This was called simply, "The Sempervirens Forest Play", and was again written by Richards with music by Howard H. Hanson, head of the music department at the College of the Pacific in San Jose and later Dean of the Rochester School of Music. A legal dispute over who owned the rights to the first play had ended the collaboration of Richards and Cator. The court later determined that Richards did. The July 1920 performance of the Forest Play attracted a large crowd, and one writer predicted that this "out-of-door spectacle, which will be given annually, will make San Jose the Oberammergau of America". However, the following year the production was canceled due to lack of money. In response to a fund-raising plea, Senator Phelan

wrote that the play would not be a financial success because of the condition of the roads into the park, and said he only donated money to "preserve the forests in Humboldt and Mendocino counties which the axman is threatening". Adding that the last performance "could hardly be considered an artistic success", Phelan nevertheless did enclose a check for $100 which was returned after the outdoor pageant was canceled.

In 1918, the Save-the-Redwoods League was organized by three scientists concerned about the destruction of the redwood groves in northern California which Phelan had pledged to help save. Dr. John C. Merriam, Professor of Paleontology at the University of California, Berkeley; Henry Fairfield Osborn, President of the American Museum of Natural History; and Madison Grant, Chairman of the New York Zoological Society, formed the League after a trip to view the deforestation in August, 1917. Over the years, the Sempervirens Club and the League have had a close working relationship, supporting each other's campaigns to save redwoods throughout California. In 1921, League Vice President Joseph Grant wrote to Sempervirens Club Secretary Alexander Murgotten, "we particularly value your surrender of your own bill to the common good. The trees along the northern highway were in imminent danger, and had we not been successful in securing the appropriation, it would have been impossible to save them". The Club had publicized a resolution to the governor backing the League's bill. The League, along with the Sierra Club, would later help to preserve endangered trees in the Santa Cruz Mountains.

At the annual meeting of the Sempervirens Club at Big Basin in 1922, Hill and Unitarian minister Charles Pease were delegated to take a trip through "the Primeval forests of the Butano" to interview property owners, and to secure options on 15,000 acres of forest. While they completed that trip and showed photographs at a Club meeting, the project to include Butano in the California Redwood Park remained unfinished at Hill's death on September 3, 1922. A month before he died at the age of sixty-nine,

Hill received a letter from Newton Drury, Secretary of the Save-the-Redwoods League in which Drury wrote "we are anxious to keep in close touch with the Sempervirens Club. It has been of inestimable value to the State in promoting the cause of saving the Redwoods".

After Andrew Hill's death, Secretary Murgotten was appointed Club President and promised to continue Hill's work to both preserve Butano Canyon, and to assist the League in the preservation of other redwood forests in the state. Hill's wife, Florence, long a Director of the Sempervirens Club, was made an honorary Vice President along with Past Presidents Charles Reed and Kate Kennedy. Andrew Hill, Jr. would later become Secretary of the Club. Andrew Hill's ashes were scattered beneath the large "Father of the Forest" redwood in California Redwood Park.

The Redwood Inn, "California Redwood Park".    *Photo: Roy Fulmer, Sempervirens Fund Collection*

South entrance to "State Redwood Park", circa 1910.    *Photo: Sempervirens Fund Collection*

# VI.

## The Club and the New State Park System

*Our Club is a semi-political organization as our accomplishments are principally attained through County, State, and National Legislation. Therefore, in a large co-operating membership, there is strength.*

**Wallace P. Isham, 1926**
**Address to Sempervirens Club Directors**

While Alexander Murgotten served as Secretary of the Sempervirens Club for many years, his tenure as President was short. Not long before his death, Hill had confided to Judge Hartman that, "Mr. Murgotten is dead as a secretary, he has made no attempt to collect dues from the members. I think it must be because he is getting so old. He must be 76 at least. We should put in a younger man and pay him a reasonable amount to keep the books of the club".

As President, Murgotten pledged to continue the work of Andrew Hill, especially in the campaign to preserve the Butano Forest as a state park, and in providing assistance to the Save-the-Redwoods League. He also reconfirmed the Semperviren's Club's commitment to encourage proper maintenance of the park, to support the building of a road to the park from the coast, to ensure that the planned Skyline Boulevard south from San Francisco was routed close to the park, and to dedicate the largest tree in the park in memory of Hill. At the Club's annual meeting in 1923, one committee was appointed to explore ways to save the Butano Forest and another one to find a suitable memorial for Andrew Hill. While Murgotten relinquished leadership of the Club after three months to S.W. Waterhouse, he continued to serve as Secretary until his own death four years later.

Waterhouse, a distributor of automotive equipment, builder's supplies, and machine tools from San Francisco, had an equally short tenure of four months as Club President. He devoted

himself to working on trails in Big Basin and compiling maps and guides for the park. The publication of one guide netted the club over $1,000, a considerable sum at that time. But there was friction with Murgotten, and Waterhouse eventually resigned as President while continuing as a Director. Over the course of the next few years, Waterhouse tendered his resignation as a Director several times stating, "I make a general practice of severing my connections with any organization in the activities of which I cannot participate to a considerable degree". Apparently the primary cause of this lack of participation was attributed to his not residing in San Jose. Despite these gestures, Waterhouse continued to serve on Club committees throughout the 1920's.

Waterhouse was replaced as President of the Sempervirens Club in May 1923, by William R. Flint who had served in the State Assembly from 1908 to 1912, and in the State Senate from 1912 until 1916. His family had large land holdings in San Benito County and in Southern California where they were partners with James Irvine. Both his uncle and cousin had been members of the State Legislature. Flint had been a supporter of the Club for over ten years and along with Senator Herbert Jones had introduced legislation for both the Saratoga and coast roads into the park.

The Sempervirens Club decided to further honor Andrew Hill's memory with a memorial water fountain. It was dedicated on Memorial Day in 1924. Senator Jones was in charge of the program. Speakers included his mother, Louise, one of the seven founders of the Sempervirens Club; President Flint and Secretary Murgotten; Redwood Commissioner Reverend Z.J. Maher, President of Santa Clara College; and John E. Richards who had been appointed a State Supreme Court Judge. Richards' wife read a poem written by former

Club President Kate Kennedy.

During the early 1920's, a movement was underway to establish a state park system in California, and the Sempervirens Club was called upon to play a part in this effort. At the national level, the protection of forests and the preservation of land in public parks had been separate since the creation of the National Park Service in 1916. Club member Charles Wing, who had become a Colonel after serving with the Twenty-third Army Engineers in France during World War I, wrote to Senator Jones that the federal government:

*has recognized the difference in needs between parks and forests and (has) therefore provided for the management of parks and forests under different departments. Forestry problems are largely problems of agriculture — of the growing and harvesting of a crop. Park problems are largely problems of public policy as concerns health, recreation and education. All the trained foresters that I have talked with acknowledge that the problems are entirely different.*

Colonel Wing told the Senator that the Club "would probably strongly object to again placing the administration of the California Redwood Park under the Forestry Board, due to the unfortunate past experience". Forestry practices that favored the production of lumber over the preservation of ancient forests had been seen as the cause of "The Rape of the Redwoods" scandal in 1908. In addition to problems of control and coordination, many citizens wanted more and bigger parks. An organization in Los Angeles calling itself the California State Parks Association wrote Jones in December 1922, that "there is no group of people at present doing the things we have in mind, namely, taking out of the market at once all the park area in the State that it is wise and desirable to save for the future before it is higher priced".

In January 1925, an important meeting was held by the State Parks Committee of the Save-the-Redwoods League at the Ferry Building on the waterfront in San Francisco. President Flint represented the Sempervirens Club along with Judge Richards and his wife. The Chairman of the Committee was Duncan McDuffie, a wealthy Bay Area developer and real estate speculator who was also President of the Sierra Club and a Director of the League. McDuffie told the gathering of businessmen, politicians,

and conservationists that Big Basin was "the only state park which can be said to have been adequately organized for use by the people of the state". Other parks were poorly managed and funded by an increasing crazy-quilt of state departments, agencies, boards, and commissions. For reasons of "efficiency, economy and sound administration", McDuffie argued, the state's public lands required the "creation of a state park commission with adequate powers and funds". In addition, preservation of the state's scenic attractions in public parks was important for tourism which was second only to agriculture in economic importance to the state. "Many of the attractions that have made the state famous are being destroyed like our redwood groves, or are passing into private ownership like the Monterey coastline", McDuffie told the meeting.

Judge Richards was noncommittal about "the present wisdom of forming a State Park Commission", but related to Murgotten that Colonel Wing "had fully approved his recommendation in that regard". The Ferry Building gathering voted to support a campaign for a state park system and a California State Parks Committee was formed. Advertising executive and League Secretary Newton Drury sent copies of McDuffie's speech throughout the state and received endorsements back from the Sempervirens Club in addition to those from the Sierra Club; the Calaveras Grove Association; the Point Lobos Association; and such national groups as the American Civic Association, American Forestry Association, the National Parks Association and the National Conference for State Parks; as well as from the Save-the-Redwoods League itself. The state's automobile club, pioneer organizations, and the California Federation of Women's Clubs were also strongly supportive. But legislation to create a park system was opposed by the giant Pacific Lumber Company and other timber interests. Additional opposition came from the influential California Development Association and from former Governor Pardee, who had dissolved the first Redwood Commission. The bill died with a "pocket veto" by Governor Friend William Richardson. The Governor, an extreme conservative who signed less than half the bills sent him, was defeated for re-election in 1926 by Clement Calhoun ("C.C.") Young, a friend and business partner of Duncan McDuffie. At a meeting attended by Sempervirens Club members at the Palace Hotel in San Francisco in February 1927, the California State Parks Committee was revived. It set about organizing what has been called "the largest publicity campaign in California's history". That year, the Legislature unanimously passed three bills which provided for a central commission to unify administration of all parks; ordered a comprehensive survey of state park possibilities; and called for a $6 million bond issue which, with matching private funds, would buy $12 million worth of land for the park system. Another piece of legislation created the Department of Natural Resources which would include both a Division of Forestry and a Division of Parks.

After signing the legislation in the summer of 1927, Governor Young appointed five men to the new Park Commission: Sierra Club activist William Colby, Stanford President Ray Lyman Wilbur, Southern California attorney Henry O'Melveny, internationally-known explorer Major Frederick Russell Burnham of Hollywood, and Senator Wilbur Chandler of Fresno. At the

Commission's first meeting in January 1928, Colonel Wing was appointed Chief of the Division of Parks. Wing, who had first mapped Big Basin in the 1880's with fellow Stanford professor William Dudley, and who had served for many years with the Redwood Park Commission, was a natural choice. In addition to serving as a Director of the Sempervirens Club since the 1920's, Wing also found time to design Stanford Stadium and to consult on the Hetch Hetchy Dam project. California Redwood Park was renamed Big Basin Redwoods State Park in 1927 with its inclusion in the new Division of Parks.

As the campaign to pass the $6 million bond issue went into high gear, Colonel Wing was one of the featured guests at a large Sempervirens Club banquet held in Big Basin in June during their annual outing. The National Conference of State Parks was holding its meeting in San Francisco and many participants came to the banquet, including State Park Commission Chairman Colby and Stephen Mather, Director

Automobile camping in "State Redwood Park", circa 1910.    *Photo: Roy Fulmer, Sempervirens Fund Collection*

of the National Park Service. The featured speaker was U.S. Congressman Arthur M. Free, a charter member of the Club. He urged the gathering to support the bond issue, and in November 1928, it passed by an overwhelming vote of three to one. In a report to the new commissioners, the Club argued for "the necessity of extending the boundaries of the Big Basin Park westward so as to include lands now held in private ownership, which are a part of the Big Basin, and are almost entirely surrounded by present Park lands". This report was obviously designed to get the attention of Frederick Law Olmsted, Jr. Olmstead was conducting a survey of state park needs and the Club's report called attention to the "many-hued waterfalls" which were not then under

Berry Creek Falls.
*Photo: Alexander Lowry, Sempervirens Fund Collection*

park ownership, and included an article from the *San Francisco Chronicle* which praised each of the three falls along Berry Creek in glowing terms — "the golden eagle in your pocket is not more

golden than the rocky steps which the Golden Falls descend". All of the land in the Big Basin should be included in the park, the Club manifesto stated. And, as if to find pragmatic and utilitarian reasons for purchasing the falls, a page was attached with statistics showing water flow and possible electrical output.

The Sempervirens Club under the leadership of both Murgotten and Flint focused efforts on achieving a western access road into the park from the coast. The report to the Park Commission had also argued for "another entrance from the West, and a road through the Park from East to West". After $10,000 was approved for an initial survey, Senator Jones lobbied heavily in Sacramento for construction, but economy-minded governors continually refused to sign bills funding a new road. Santa Clara lawmakers had won their long battle for an eastern access road and were disinclined to offer support for another road that would permit visitors to bypass their attractions and businesses. The only way Jones was able to finally secure approval from Governor C.C. Young for the road along Gazos Creek was to call it a "fire escape road". According to a circular letter from President Flint, the "Park constitutes a menace to visitors by reason of the possibility of forest fires". The only two roads into the park were from the east, Flint wrote, and the previous year, a fire jumped both roads. "With a strong wind and a rapidly traveling fire, and with burning logs falling across the road, campers in the Park would be completely trapped...The mind cannot picture the holocaust if a forest fire were to cut off the present exits!" Newton Drury, Secretary of the Save-the-Redwoods League, wrote that the "League will be very glad to cooperate with you in urging the construction of the 'fire escape' road".

In addition to the western road campaign, the Club published a booklet, *Unto the Children: A Story of the Redwoods*, authored by San Jose writer Austin Hall. The story of a journey by a widowed Vermont lumberman from Los Gatos into the Santa Cruz Mountains redwoods with his seven-year-old daughter, it was first published in nationally-circulated *Everybody's Magazine* and was then donated by the author to help in fund-raising efforts by the Sempervirens Club. In a letter accompanying the booklet, Flint confessed that the Club was "in need of a little money to continue the fight to 'Save the Redwoods'." In Hall's tale, on their way to see the famous redwoods, the lumberman and his daughter meet up with the legendary Mountain Charlie McKiernan who helped them purchase 80 acres where the man cut down one ancient tree to build an entire hotel. Years later, the lumberman turned-hotel proprietor agreed to take care of the "frail, delicate, pampered" son of a visiting capitalist one summer in order to toughen him up. After growing up, the son returned at the last moment to save the few remaining trees from the destruction threatened by his father's logging company. Flint wrote to Club members that the story would help "to inculcate a love for the redwoods, and for outdoor life", and would no doubt increase membership revenue. In a postscript, Flint added that "if you are interested in this great humanitarian work of saving these magnificent trees for future generations, send us a liberal check to aid us in our work".

The redwood forest preservation movement was growing, but with national attention and money focused on saving the redwoods north of San Francisco. A note of discouragement crept into Flint's correspondence. In January, 1926, he stated, "Sometimes I wonder if the efforts of the Club would be more effective if we joined the 'Save the Redwoods League,' but again it seems better that we should keep our individuality as we have done, thereby functioning locally and more effectively". The suggestion of a merger had also been made by Murgotten to League Secretary Drury. In his response, Drury paid tribute to the uniqueness of the Sempervirens Club:

*I personally am inclined to believe that you should surely keep the Sempervirens Club in existence. It has a record of splendid achievements, and there are likely to arise any number of questions upon which its voice should be heard. You have been most helpful in cooperating with the Save the Redwoods League at all times.*

Drury added that he would be glad to discuss the possibility of a merger, but after the mid-1920's, the issue was never raised again.

At the nadir of the Club's fortunes, Murgotten died and Flint resigned as president to pursue land development interests in Southern California. Wallace Isham, a San Jose insurance salesman, was elected President at the end of 1926, and prospects looked bleak.

Owing to the passing of our faithful Secretary, Alex P. Murgotten, soon after the 1926 annual meeting, the writer found himself practically without support, with no program ahead and unable to obtain a quorum for a directors meeting, owing to the fact that some were living away, others were out of town and with resignations pending from others. Some were disinterested to the extent that the Club's future existence hung in a balance.

Isham, with a promoter's zeal unequaled since Hill's time, soon organized a gala celebration to mark the 20th anniversary of the Club's incorporation in 1907. In a letter to the new Board of Directors, which includes Herbert Jones and his mother Louise; Judge Richards, Colonel Wing; Judge James Welch, who owned land in the Castle Rock area west of San Jose; and Andrew P. Hill, Jr., Isham bragged that "interest is apparently gathering momentum, and there are before us some important matters to be considered", namely:

*the matter of developing the Club properties adjoining the Big Basin Park, and the erection of a Club house or Sempervirens Camp. The acquisition of additional redwood properties, together with new road construction, fire prevention, etc., as well as building up an exclusive membership of interested citizens.*

Isham reminded the directors that the Sempervirens Club, "is a semi-political organization as our accomplishments are principally attained through County, State, and National legislation. Therefore, in a large co-operating membership, there is strength". Besides acquiring additional groves of redwoods, Isham proposed a reforestation project for land subjected to fire. To achieve these objectives, the new president suggested "an active publicity campaign through a huge membership drive", and asked that the Directors consider affiliating with other similar organizations, perhaps including the Save-the-Redwoods League and the Sierra Club.

At the 20th anniversary meeting held at the Sainte Claire Hotel in San Jose, the featured speaker was Duncan McDuffie who was then attempting to persuade the Legislature to pass the park bill sponsored by his California State Parks Committee. Senator Jones spoke to the membership about the fire escape road and Judge Welch, whose favored project was the proposed Skyline Boulevard in the hills through his property, lectured "on topics of especial interest to lovers of the park". After the ceremonies, everyone removed to Bakesto Park, in northeast San Jose, where two redwood trees were planted and dedicated in memory of Hill and Murgotten — "our departed friends and most faithful co-workers". Isham said that the day was, "one of the most memorable occasions in the Club's history, and it is hoped all received an inspiration to press on with a more vigorous spirit than ever, that wonderful work of saving the redwoods, not only from the ruthless hand of man but from the ravages of fire". Over the years, more memorial trees were added to the Sempervirens Club grove in Bakesto Park. In 1932, trees were planted for Judge Welch; Louise Jones; Kate Kennedy; Park Warden William Dool; William Lyon, business manager for the *San Jose Mercury*; and Mattie Murgotten. In 1935, trees were planted for Judge Isaiah Hartman and David Satterthwait; and in 1940, for Mrs. A.T. Herrmann and Club founder, W. W. Richards. Isham himself was memorialized with a tree in 1946.

Following the 1927 celebration, Isham heard from Fred McPherson, editor of the *Santa Cruz Sentinel* and son of Duncan McPherson who had been present at the Stanford meeting on May 1, 1900. "You certainly had a good meeting", McPherson told him, "and deserve much credit for starting a movement to include within the park area several units of land necessary to the protection of the park". During the next few months, there were excursions of Club members to the property in Big Basin donated by I.T. Bloom years before for an encampment, and into the Butano where, according to the new Club Secretary, Andrew Hill, Jr., former President Waterhouse suggested a temporary camp could be built prior to "starting an agitation for its preservation". Isham traveled to San Francisco to discuss the availability of land with Timothy Hopkins, one of the largest landowners in San Mateo and Santa Cruz counties, and predicted that "there will soon be a first class bus line running into the Basin from Santa Cruz". Hopkins had been a silent partner of Middleton, who sold the original park to the state. In a letter to the *Chronicle* in 1936 after Hopkins' death, Charles Wesley Reed paid tribute to his essential role in obtaining that land before it was logged.

At a 1928 barbecue hosted by the Sempervirens Club for guests at the 8th National Conference on State Parks in Big Basin, new State Park Commissioner William Colby paid tribute to the Club's twenty-eight years of work on behalf of the redwoods:

*We owe a great debt of gratitude to this club, because this great park we have here would probably by this time have been destroyed and laid low if it had not been for the work of these men and women. I can remember the great battle it took to get this legislation through for the purchase of this grove. Many people then could not see the value of preserving it. But I know that now we can all recognize and agree that the move was one of the wisest moves ever made in the state of California, to have this glorious park preserved here and these great trees.*

The barbecue was served to nearly 200 members of the Club and their guests beneath the redwoods and huge oaks of the park. According to the *San Jose Mercury Herald*, "the music, as announced by the menus, was furnished by the trees. Bluejays, chattering overhead and boldly approaching the tables for tidbits, and deer walking about unafraid, added a delightful touch to the meal".

A review of the membership list of the Sempervirens Club from May 1927, provides an idea of the character of the membership at that time. In addition to individuals and couples on the typed list of 405 names, there were thirty-seven institutional memberships including a dozen banks, an equal number of businesses, four hotels, five women's clubs, and Santa Clara College. Of the readily identifiable businesses, there were a lumber company, tannery, market, hardware store, paper company, and the San Jose Water Works. Most of the members lived in the region stretching from San Francisco to Santa Cruz, with the largest number residing in the San Jose area. One member lived in Seattle; a few were from Southern California; and Edwin Markham, the San Jose writer who had achieved phenomenal fame with his poem "The Man With a Hoe", which had been published in the *San Francisco Examiner* in 1899, was then living in New York. There were twenty-six doctors, a sprinkling of attorneys, and seven judges. Many of the San Franciscans on the list were prominent in their professional fields:

Senator James Phelan; Mayor James Rolph; sugar heir Rudolph Spreckles; financiers Henry Cowell, William Crocker, H.L. Tevis, and Timothy Hopkins; Park Commissioner William Colby; Parks Director Colonel Charles Wing; and Duncan McDuffie, Chairman of the State Parks Committee. Big Basin Warden Billy Dool was on the list, along with park concessionaire Roy Fulmer and his wife. Also included were *Santa Cruz Sentinel* publisher Duncan McPherson and former Lt. Governor William Jeter, both of whom had attended the Stanford meeting in May, 1900. Congressmember Arthur Free was on the 1927 list, as were Everis A. Hayes and Jay O. Hayes, owners of the *San Jose Mercury* and politicians who served both in Sacramento and Washington. And finally there were the Club stalwarts: Louise and Herbert Jones, Kate Kennedy, Mattie Murgotten, Mrs. A.T. Hermann, William Flint, Dr. James Bullitt, Judge Isaiah Hartman, W.S. Rodgers of the *Boulder Creek Mountain Echo*, and Hill's widow Florence and son Andrew, Jr. There were 161 names on the list marked "paid". Of these, fifty-three were women and six were institutions. Membership cards during this period contained the following oath: "I pledge allegiance to the Sempervirens Club and the principles for which it stands: To save the Redwoods from the ravages of fire and the ruthless hand of man."

While Isham was able to hold the Club together during the Depression years, his high hopes for expanding the park's boundaries could not produce tangible results. In 1929, the Sempervirens Club decided to celebrate the 29th anniversary of its founding with a barbecue in Big Basin. The May event was to include members of conservation groups from Central Coast and San Joaquin counties as well as Park Commissioners. The menu featured seafood, "Filet of Toro", and "Frijoles Espanole", along with "Chili Salsa" and "Java Royal." In 1932, the club celebrated the 25th anniversary of its incorporation with a luncheon and the planting of additional redwoods for deceased members in Bakesto Park. The featured speaker was Winfield Scott, a former member of the State Board of Forestry and manager of the Butano State Park Association who indicated that the preservation of the Butano Forest continued to be part of the Club's plans for a "greater" Big Basin park.

The on-going role of the clergy in preservation efforts was reinforced at the 35th anniversary celebration of the founding of the Club in 1935. The Reverend James J. Lyons, S.J., President of Santa Clara College, said in his invocation that the redwood groves, God's first temples, "are among the most humbling of nature's marvels to men not entirely encased in self conceit". He added that "it is a solace to consider that the venerable giants antedate the Christian era by many centuries".

The Butano campaign got a big boost in 1940

Waddell Beach, Rancho del Oso and Big Basin beyond.
*Photo: Alexander Lowry, Sempervirens Fund Collection*

as the Sempervirens Club celebrated forty years of saving the redwoods. As early as 1931, Isham had written to the *San Francisco Examiner* complimenting it for an editorial advocating that Butano be included in a state park; "Mr. Hearst's ambition towards the preservation of the forest and wilderness are well known". At the 40th anniversary gathering, Club members resolved to find $50,000 to match a state appropriation that was to come either from oil revenues or from horse racing receipts for the purchase of approximately 1,000 acres of virgin forest surrounding Berry Creek Falls, long a target of both loggers and preservationists and not far from the southern edge of the vast Butano region. This goal was supported by Newton Drury, now acquisition agent for the Park Commission as well as Secretary of the Save-the-Redwoods League. Other speakers at the Club event included the Reverend Francis Caffrey of San Juan Bautista, newest member of the State Park Commission; Fred McPherson, Jr. and Dr. Thomas MacQuarrie, the presidents of the Santa Cruz and San Jose Chambers of Commerce; and representatives of the San Lorenzo Valley Property Owners Club, the Contra Costa County Development Association, and the Pomona Grange, among others. Winfield Scott, a leader in the Butano movement, expressed the view that the park should eventually extend "from the skyline to the sea", a vision that was finally realized over a quarter century later with the trail by that name. Bert Werder, a San Mateo County fire warden, told the gathering that the entire Santa Cruz Mountains should be saved as a vast playground for the San Francisco metropolitan area, a view echoing the dreams of Sempervirens Club founders.

"Semper Fidelis", paraphrased the *San Jose Mercury* in backing the plan:

> *Forty years ago this spring a determined little band of San Jose folk undertook to convince an indifferent public and apathetic legislature that the glorious redwoods in the Big Basin region should not be laid waste under the logger's axe... North of Big Basin lies a vast region of virgin redwood equally beautiful, far less known to the public*

Taking the stagecoach to Big Basin, circa 1890.    *Photo: Sempervirens Fund Collection*

*than the present park groves. It is the Butano, mysterious, magnificent, remote.*

The Butano was threatened now just as the Big Basin had been forty years earlier, warned the *Mercury*. "It would behoove every person who loves the redwoods, who has admired the beauty and felt the inspiration of the Big Basin groves, to take part in this new fight to keep forever unspoiled the last remnants of California's departed forest glory". The *San Jose News*, in supporting the Butano campaign, headlined its editorial the "New Crusade" and said that "some of the founders of the old Sempervirens Club are gone but the spirit of the pioneer group has lived on and burns brightly among the present membership". The editorial predicted that "it is a safe bet that the new crusade will be as successful as was the old one". In 1943, the Park Commission allocated $50,000 from the prior legislative appropriations of 1941 for matching funds to acquire Berry Creek additions to Big Basin. But it would be many years before that land would finally become part of the park. While land in the nearby Pescadero watershed was purchased from the Shriners in 1945 and became Portola State Park, Butano was not added to the park system until 1956.

Wallace Isham died in 1945 and his place as president of the Sempervirens Club, was taken by Herbert Jones. Jones had spent nearly a half century supporting the Club and working behind the scenes as Club attorney and secretary. Isham's service to the Club during his eighteen-year tenure did not result in the saving of the Butano, or a public highway from the coast, or a noticeable increase in the size of Big Basin Redwoods State Park as it was renamed by the State Park Commission in 1928. However, his drive and perseverance enabled the band of redwood preservationists in the Sempervirens Club to survive and maintain their urgent insistence that all endangered redwoods in the Santa Cruz Mountains be owned by the public, and not cut down for private profit.

Backpackers enjoy the view from Castle Rock State Park.    *Photo: Sempervirens Fund Collection*

Butterfly.
*Photo: Howard King, Sempervirens Fund Collection*

Tiger Lilly.
*Photo: Howard King, Sempervirens Fund Collection*

Five Finger Fern.
*Photo: Howard King, Sempervirens Fund Collection*

Young lady with a handful of
bright yellow banana slugs.
*Photo: Gil Hernandez,
Private Collection*

# VII.

## The Butano Forest Campaign

*The majesty of the redwoods, the beauty of the streams lined with azaleas and ferns, the charm of the potreros fringed with tiger lilies – all these cast a spell over me that has never ceased.*

Herbert Jones

"I recall my first summer in the Big Basin", Herbert Jones wrote to W.S. Rodgers in the early 1940's. "I was still in college. Mr. A.P. Hill gave me my summer vacation with the Sempervirens Club in return for my going over a couple of weeks in advance and helping to get the camp in shape". Herbert Jones was a law student at Stanford at the time. Herbert and his brother Augustine had fished with Hill and had worked as "baggage slingers and roustabouts" helping other campers by carrying their gear, packing in water, and helping put up their tents.

*The territory seemed very wild and unexplored. The majesty of the redwoods, the beauty of the streams lined with azaleas and ferns, the charm of the potreros fringed with tiger lilies — all these cast a spell over me that has never ceased.*

In his retirement from editing the *Boulder Creek Mountain Echo*, Rodgers had been one of the strongest supporters of the idea of a park in Big Basin. Congratulating him on his ninetieth birthday, Jones reminded him of "the apathy you had to overcome of those who thought our forests were limitless, and the opposition of those who only saw in the magnificent monarchs of the forest an opportunity for enormous financial profits."

The battle to establish a "people's park" in Big Basin did not end with the purchase of the land in 1902. It required the continuing efforts of individuals like Rodgers and Jones to campaign for access roads into the park and for the addition of land in the Waddell Creek watershed to fulfill the Sempervirens Club founders' original vision of a "greater park" in the Santa Cruz Mountains. The role of Herbert Jones has not been well documented, although he devoted much of his life to the work of the Sempervirens Club. In addition to his early involvement, he served as president from 1945 until the Club's incorporation papers were turned over to the newly-formed Sempervirens Fund in 1968. While Hill and the other founders had the vision that brought the park into existence, Jones was foremost among the managers and administrators who contributed to the Sempervirens Club's longevity.

Herbert Jones' public reputation is based not so much on his work on behalf of the redwoods, but on his long career as a state legislator and for the critical role that he played in developing California's water resources. In 1913, he was elected to the State Senate from San Jose where he had been practicing as an attorney for the previous six years. According to Andrew Hill, much of the credit for Jones' election belonged to support from Sempervirens Club members. Jones repaid that debt by obtaining an appropriation of $70,000 from the State for the Saratoga road to Big Basin which opened in 1915. Because of a cross-filing loophole in the election that year, Jones set a record never since equaled by running on four tickets — Republican, Democratic, Progressive and Prohibitionist – and winning on all of them.

Jones was actually a Progressive Republican. He was an important legislative leader in the reform-era administration of Governor Hiram Johnson, and he was rumored to have been a potential candidate for Governor himself. An editorial in his hometown newspaper declared him the "politician of the century" in Santa Clara County. He was President of the Progressive Voters League between 1923 and 1926 when it helped to successfully defeat conservative Republican Governor Friend W. Richardson, and elect progressive Republican C.C. Young.

Jones was also a pious teetotaler. Many of the California laws implementing Prohibition were his handiwork. The "Jones anti-still bill" made possession of a still, or the parts thereof, a felony. Among the other issues that Jones championed were education and water. In education, he was involved in efforts to convert the old normal schools to state colleges and was instrumental in establishing the system of junior colleges in California. But it was in water legislation that Jones made his mark. A large framed print of Frederic Remington's celebrated painting, "Fight for the Water Hole", hung in his San Jose law office and it symbolized his approach to the water problem. "More than any other single individual", wrote one local historian, "Herb Jones was responsible for bringing water to the Santa Clara Valley — enough water to meet the needs of an urban metropolis". Another writer called him, "Father of Waters". As Chairman of the Senate Committee on Public Health in one of the early sessions of his service in the legislature, he introduced and secured the passage of legislation for a Sanitary Commission to have jurisdiction over the fresh-water streams of the state. He was a member of the Senate group that in 1928 prepared an amendment to the state constitution whereby the "riparian" right to water was restricted to the reasonable use of water by reasonable methods. Jones introduced an enabling bill that, after two failed attempts, ultimately became the Water Conservation Act of 1931. This created the legal framework for the old Santa Clara Valley Water Conservation District, predecessor of the current water district, and for similar agencies throughout the state.

Throughout his long service to the county and state, Jones continued to represent the Sempervirens Club and fight for important membership issues like the western access road. The voluminous correspondence he left behind in various university archives show that he worked tirelessly with the Sierra Club, the Save-the-Redwoods League, and other conservation organizations to save threatened forests in the Santa Cruz Mountains — in Big Basin as well as in the Butano and Pescadero watersheds to the north.

Another longtime member of the Club was Colonel Charles Wing, who died in 1945. Jones chose Ernest Dudley, nephew of the late Stanford botanist William Dudley who had played a major part in the early campaign, to replace Wing as a

Club director. In his letter to Dudley, Jones said that the Sempervirens Club "is reorganizing to throw its efforts into the movement to save the Butano Forest". After a visit with the Sierra Club in the Pescadero watershed, Jones wrote a letter to Parks Chief A.E. Henning stating that "the trees are falling" there and asking for Henning's support to save the redwoods in that area. From Boulder Creek, W.S. Rodgers wrote Jones that he was "very glad that you have decided to continue the Butano forest campaign. The greatest part of it has and is now being destroyed by the mill men."

Aubrey Drury, Newton's brother and Administrative Secretary for the Save-the-Redwoods League, sent Jones his support "for the program for saving timber in the Pescadero and Butano region," and discussed the legislature's appropriation of $10 million for seacoast beaches and $5 million for the purchase of other lands for parks inland. The main problem with this legislation was a technicality that prevented Butano from receiving funds because it was too far inland to be a beach, but could not qualify as an "interior" park because San Mateo County bordered the ocean. Drury said the interpretation of the bill's wording was largely in the hands of the State Park Commission.

Jones represented the Sempervirens Club at a December 1945 meeting in Redwood City with representatives of the State Chamber of Commerce, American Legion, Peninsula Women's Clubs, the Horsemen's Association, the Eagles, Supervisors from San Mateo and four other counties, and others who had organized into the "Statewide Committee for Acquisition of the Butano". "We want an interpretation", Jones told that gathering, "as to whether Butano Forest, situated five miles from the coast, may be construed as an 'interior area'." San Mateo's leaders announced that they would include their San Mateo County Park, which had been purchased for $70,000 and later received $75,000 worth of improvements, as part of matching money required for transfer of Butano to the state park system. At the request of American Legion representatives, the meeting resolved that when it was acquired, the Butano Forest area would be named, "Veterans Memorial Park", in honor of World War II veterans. Among the resolutions adopted by the committee was one urging Governor Earl Warren to include on his agenda for a special session of the legislature

Along Gazos Creek in the Butano forest.    *Photo: Frank Balthis, Sempervirens Fund Collection*

an amendment to the park appropriation bill allowing Butano to be included for funding. In a letter to the Governor, Jones said that "even as I write the trees are crashing" in the Butano, and asked Warren to help "break the log-jam and make it possible for steps quickly to be taken to acquire this forest as a state park". He added that he had "hiked through this Butano region in summers past, and hence feel personally acquainted with the beauties of its timber and its advantages, and the urgent need for it as a recreational outlet for the increasing population of the Bay Region". Governor Warren replied that while he was "very much interested in the acquisition of additional State Parks", it was not an appropriate matter to be discussed at the upcoming special session which was restricted to other pressing issues. Despite Warren's hesitancy, the Legislature did clarify the matter according to the committee's resolution and the State Park Commission ordered a survey of the Butano.

Jones also sought support for preservation from state labor leaders. In one letter he argued that the state parks are "a God send (sic) to working people. They furnish wholesome recreation, and the opportunity for family picnics free of cost. They also furnish sites for camping and wood for cooking for a nominal charge". This language was reminiscent of that used by Father Kenna and Reverend Williams in their pleas that Big Basin be a "people's park" where citizens of the Bay Area could find rest and relaxation away from the trials and tribulations of modern urban civilization.

Butano remained on the agenda of the Sempervirens Club. At the annual meeting in March 1946, San Mateo County Fire Warden Bert Werder again addressed the group, reporting on the progress of the survey of the Butano forest. Frederick Law Olmsted, Jr., appraiser for the State Park Commission, conducted the survey for the purpose of recommending that part of Butano be acquired by the state. Olmsted had also indicated the possible connection of Big Basin, Butano, and the redwood groves in the Pescadero drainage, owned since 1924 by the Islam Temple Shrine of San Francisco. (After the meeting, a tree was planted in Bakesto Park in San Jose to honor the late Club President Isham, making a total of thirteen memorial trees planted for deceased Club officials.) In June, the Club sponsored a "motor caravan excursion" of more than one hundred people into the Butano Forest for a picnic and discussion of the area's natural resources. The trip was co-sponsored by the State Chamber of Commerce, the San Mateo Planning Commission and the Loma Prieta Chapter of the Sierra Club. In addition to Jones and Werder, speakers included A.E. Connick, Chairman of the State Chamber of Commerce Committee on Resources and L.G. Barrett, Secretary of the Hollister Irrigation District and the Pacheco Pass Water District. Guests learned that the land for the park had been purchased in 1945 by the Pacific Lumber Company of Humboldt County which now had it priced at $2 million. This was the same land that had been donated to Stanford University by Timothy Hopkins, but had been sold to raise funds for the school.

During the trip, Jones announced a new Sempervirens Club campaign to rename the Shriners Grove, called Portola State Park after the state purchased it from the Shriners the year before, in honor of Chris Iverson. Iverson, a Scandinavian immigrant who had worked as a Pony Express rider and shotgun guard, had acquired two parcels of land on Pescadero Creek in the 1860's. His cabin remained on the property until it fell during the earthquake of 1989. In early years, travelers by horseback from Stanford stayed overnight at the Iverson ranch on their way to and from the Big Basin. The idea to change the name had originated with Ashley Browne, stepson of Colonel Wing. Herbert Jones agreed that Iverson was a more suitable

name than Portola, the Spaniard who explored up and down the Peninsula but who did not visit the Pescadero watershed. This campaign did not garner much support, however. Santa Cruz attorney Emmet C. Rittenhouse, a member of the Native Sons of the Golden West, told Jones that he found no one who knew anything about Chris Iverson, "or anything that he had done with regard to the redwoods of this county". He said that he could think of more appropriate people to honor. "I find the consensus of opinion is that if the name of the Park is to be changed it should be changed to 'Colonel Chas. B. Wing State Park' or 'Winfred Scott Rodgers State Park'."

In July 1946, a ceremony was held in Big Basin to rededicate the Andrew Hill tablet and drinking fountain which had been moved due to park construction. It had been relocated to the Redwood Trail near the "Father of the Forest", which was the largest of the park's ancient redwoods and Andrew Hill's final resting place. More than two hundred people attended the festivities, and the first person to drink out of the new fountain was the widow of W.S. Rodgers. In addition to Jones, who paid tribute to Hill as "the man who saved the redwoods", Chairman of the State Park Commission, Joseph Knowland, told of the growth of the state park system which now comprised eighty parks and nineteen monuments. Although Charles Wesley Reed, first President of the Sempervirens Club,

The Andrew P. Hill Fountain, Big Basin, July 1946.    *Photo: Clyde Arbuckle, Sempervirens Fund Collection*

was unable to attend the ceremony, he wrote to Jones from his farm near Chico that Big Basin pictures taken by Hill "hang on my walls. I take pride in the accomplishment they record, and enjoy the pleasant memories they invoke. It is highly appropriate that your mother's son should be President of the Club".

Frederick Law Olmsted, Jr., who had conducted a complete survey of all of California's existing and potential state park land in 1928, concluded in a November 1946 report that there is "no doubt whatever that (Butano) is scenically the best as well as the largest body of primeval forest remaining in this part of the state". He considered it remarkable that "large tracts of virgin redwood forest should have survived uncut for so many years just here, less than 50 miles from the midst of the enormously expanding population of the San Francisco Bay urban aggregation, and close to the starting place from which wholesale commercial logging of redwoods spread so widely and so fast". His 1928 survey had recognized the progressively growing need for nearby forest parks, due to population pressure, and recommended adding 12,000 acres to Big Basin, including Butano. Big Basin and Muir Woods were already becoming overcrowded, and if access to virgin redwood forests close to urban centers was desired, then "it will only be by prompt action in this district and only at high monetary cost", Olmsted concluded. The Sempervirens Club became a sponsor of a new organization — the Butano Forest Associates — along with the Sierra Club, Save-the-Redwoods League, the Tamalpais Conservation Club, Marin Conservation League, Mission Trails Association, the Isaac Walton League of America, and other regional and state civic organizations. Herbert Jones was a member of the board of directors of the Butano Forest Associates.

Although the 1946 Olmsted report argued forcefully for the purchase of 5,000 acres for a state park in Butano, Jones found it necessary to agitate continuously over the next few years for the purchase of park land. Big Basin Ranger Harriett Weaver, whose animal stories long delighted youngsters visiting the park, wrote an invective entitled, "Save the Butano!" for *Westways* magazine. "I hope the Butano project is coming along", she wrote in a letter to Jones along with drafts of the article for his comments.

"You must be a reader of John Muir", he commented, for "your language evinces his same passionate fondness for nature, and also the giving of personality to the trees, ferns and mountains". In reviewing her draft of an article about Andrew Hill, Jones suggested that she give credit to Father Kenna rather than the Catholic Church. "Mr. Hill seemed to stand in awe of the power of the Catholic Church", Jones said, and he mentioned it so repeatedly in his campaigns for the park and the access roads "that people came to me to have him 'pipe down'." Also, according to Jones, it was not certain that Phelan was a nephew of Kenna's, but he thought the Mayor and Senator may have only referred to him as "Uncle Robert" out of fondness. Weaver had wondered if a publisher like the Stanford University Press would be interested in a "complete story" of Big Basin and the Sempervirens Club. Jones responded that if she should decide "to write a full history of the movement for the preservation of the Big Basin, I think there are still enough old timers to give you considerable authentic information".

In 1948, an article in a magazine published by the National League For Woman's Service called for "immediate action" to preserve about 4,500 acres in the Butano. "Recreation sites are lessening with increasing home developments and ruthless lumber companies are rapidly denuding wooded areas with tragic effects. In fact, mills are running to capacity in and around the Butano Forest at present. Smaller ones carry on the destruction after the larger operators remove the big timber". The article further implored:

*Let us revive the true spirit of the Indian word BOOT-ah-noh (written at present Butano) meaning "a gathering place for friendly visits." May Butano State Park speedily become a reality and sanctuary for those seeking the quiet, peace and inspiration of the forest primeval.*

The State Park Commission had set aside funds to purchase land on a matching basis, and San Mateo County was prepared to donate valuable local park facilities to the state for this purpose. It was hoped that other surrounding counties would budget money for the Butano Park which was intended as a living memorial to World War II service men and women. Richard Leonard, President of the Sierra Club, wrote to the California War Memorial Park

Association that while his club was not directing the program for the preservation of the Butano Forest, it was "actively supporting both that project and the Calaveras pines and big trees". He urged the group to contact Jones and the Butano Forest Associates, and recommended the *Sierra Club Bulletin* which was publishing an article about the campaign in its January 1950 issue. Land in Butano was finally purchased by the state in 1956, and the park opened to the public in 1961.

Another issue occupied Jones and the Sempervirens Club members during the next fifteen years. Some of the most spectacular scenery in the Waddell Creek watershed was known to be along Berry Creek where a series of three waterfalls – Golden, Cascade and Silver – join Berry Creek Falls in the stream's 500 foot rush to join with the west fork of the Waddell. The area had long been the destination of hikers and the subject of photographers. The owner of the land thought the state should purchase his property because it would provide "a perfect dam site" for the Hoover estate, between Big Basin and the Coast, which had been targeted for eventual state ownership. "Prompt and vigorous action is necessary to save the Berry Creek region", Jones wrote to a number of possible supporters in the fall of 1946 when it was learned that the land had been sold to a San Jose contractor who planned to erect a mill and cut timber on the land. According to Jones, the State Park Commission had approved the acquisition of the Berry Creek area as an addition to the Big Basin and had set aside $50,000 to be matched by outside contributions. The Sempervirens Club had withdrawn from an earlier campaign directed by Winfield Scott to raise this money because according to Jones, "his arrangement called for commissions for himself...(and) the Sempervirens Club has never participated in any movement where a cut was going to a private individual, but has always insisted that the entire proceeds of any campaign with which it was connected for park enlargement, should go directly for land purchase". In any event, Scott's campaign failed and the Park Commission funds reverted back to the state's General Fund. Jones hoped that a movement could be started among prominent Santa Cruz landowners who "might contribute areas sufficient to make up the matching property" for the Berry Creek land. He identified prominent

citizens "whose fortunes were made in the lumbering operations", and proposed that the addition be made as "a memorial to W.S. Rodgers or to the Santa Cruz County Service Men of World War II." His chief concern seemed to be the timing of this acquisition in relation to the Club's efforts in the Butano Forest:

*This crisis has broken at the time the Sempervirens Club and allied organizations are organizing for the big drive to save the Butano timber. For that reason I am wondering whether the saving of the Berry Creek region cannot be undertaken by Santa Cruz County.*

The 1950's proved to be a frustrating and stressful decade for the Club. The quandary over redwood land in Butano and along Berry Creek had still not been resolved by 1952, when Big Basin Redwoods State Park celebrated its 50th anniversary. Jones was the principal speaker at the "Old Timers Night" ceremonies which included many older park rangers who had gotten their start in Big Basin. Guests included Everett Powell, Chief Land Procurement Officer for State Parks; Earl Hanson, Assistant Chief of California State Parks; Clyde Newlin, a district superintendent with State Parks; Fred Moody, former Chief Ranger of Big Basin; Fred Canham, retired Chief Ranger at Morro Bay; C.L. (Roy) Cushing, Chief Ranger at Seacliff State Beach; Robert Crawford, Chief Ranger at New Brighton Beach State Park; and Elmer Crawford, the park's oldest civilian employee. Mrs. Frank Clement, daughter of Tom Maddock who built the first cabin in Big Basin and wife of the San Lorenzo Valley County Supervisor, was a special guest.

In 1956, Andrew Hill was again honored for saving the redwoods when a high school in southeast San Jose was named after him. His painting of the Big Basin redwood called "Father of the Forest" was donated to the school and now hangs in its library.

While a portion of the Butano was saved by the mid-1950's, the dilemma of Berry Creek remained. In 1961, Jones headed a delegation of citizens from Santa Cruz and San Jose, including Kurt Monning of Santa Clara, Mrs. Kenneth Carpenter and David Meeker of Saratoga, and Mrs. Alice Wilder and Thomas McHugh of Santa Cruz, who met with Governor Edmund Brown to discuss the situation. By this time, the land being sought was 514 acres owned by Big Creek Timber Company and the selling price was a reported $1.5 million. While Governor Brown did not promise the necessary funds in addition to the $500,000 already available, he did direct Natural Resources Director Dewitt Nelson to contact Attorney General Stanley Mosk at once and get purchase negotiations under way. One possibility discussed was preservation of a "corridor" of uncut trees across the Big Creek holdings to join two separated areas already within the park boundaries. According to Jones, the Governor felt that condemnation proceedings were possible.

In a follow-up letter to the State Division of Beaches and Parks, Jones recounted his efforts on behalf of the Sempervirens Club in Big Basin:

*During my first session in the State Senate in 1913, I backed the bill for the $70,000 appropriation to build a state road from Saratoga Summit into the Park. In the 1917 session, I authored the bill for an appropriation of $150,000, to acquire an additional 1200 acres to protect the water supply for the Park. In the 1927 session, I presented the measure for the construction of the Gazos Creek Road.*

During all of these campaigns, Jones said, there were objections that these measures would increase taxes and impose an unduly heavy financial burden on the state. "The State has paid an appalling price, in its acquisition of park lands, because of the fear of high taxes", Jones argued. When Timothy Hopkins owned land in the Butano, 5,000 acres could be purchased for $300,000. "Year after year was allowed to slip by and finally (in 1956) the State acquired some 2,000 acres for $1.2 million". With reference to the Berry Creek lands, "the process of skyrocketing of prices has gone on continuously", Jones said, pointing out that redwood and fir were selling for thirty-five dollars per thousand board feet, up from three to four dollars per thousand board feet twelve years before.

Jones and the Club held that the ultimate aim of conservation "would be to have the State acquire all the lands along Berry Creek and its tributaries so as to round out the Park and make a contiguous or unified holding". By the time Jones was making this plea to the State, the original vision that the founders of the Sempervirens Club held of a "greater park" in the Santa Cruz Mountains of from 45,000 to 60,000 acres had faded from view. Decades of fighting over scraps of land, redwood tree by redwood tree, and the accumulation of all unsaved old-growth trees in private hands, had made this grand dream seem impossible. It would take another generation and a new incarnation of the Club, for this dream to be realized.

Gazos Creek in the Butano forest.    *Photo: Frank Balthis, Sempervirens Fund Collection*

# VIII.

## The Sempervirens Fund: Lobbying Thrust to Land Trust

*I saw what happened when they bought trees for a park, but not the watershed. Logging and fires caused erosion below and trees started falling. Then I saw that development was beginning in the Santa Cruz Mountains and the same thing could happen.*

**Tony Look, founding Executive Director of the Sempervirens Fund, 1971**

With the addition of unclaimed land in the Waddell Creek watershed through a federal grant, Big Basin Redwoods had doubled in size by 1916. Sempervirens Club stalwart Judge Isaiah Hartman had donated 200 acres of his land. In 1920, Senator Jones secured $150,000 in appropriations from the Legislature to purchase another 1,200 acres from two lumber companies. In the late 1920's and early 1930's, an additional 500 acres came into state ownership through gifts and small appropriations. Lumberman H.L. Middleton's estate deeded 910 acres over to the state for the park in 1955, in addition to an earlier donation of five acres for a warden's cottage. In 1959, the Sempervirens Club transferred to the State the four and one-half acres that I.T. Bloom had earlier given to the Club for a campground which had remained unused and undeveloped. While Big Basin was of moderate size for a state park, it remained much smaller than the "greater park" that Sempervirens Club founder Carrie Stevens Walter, Stanford botanist William Dudley, and others had envisioned over fifty years before when they urged that all of the forested watershed in the Santa Cruz Mountains be preserved. 10,000 acres in the Waddell Creek watershed remained in private hands, and as the price of lumber rose following World War II, the economic impetus to log the big trees increased.

From its founding in 1900, the Sempervirens Club had primarily been a lobbying organization and had achieved considerable success towards its goals because of its political connections, not the least of which were State Senators Jones and Flint, and U.S. Congressmember Free. Andrew P. Hill had been able to raise over $7,000 in contributions from generous donors towards the purchase price of a right-of-way from Saratoga Gap into the park, but the Club's fund-raising efforts otherwise had been limited. Members paid one dollar a year in dues and this money went towards circular letters to promote preservation issues and annual events. In the spirit of the times, Club members looked to government to pay for saving the redwoods. When economy-minded administrations declined to help them, they explored other strategies, as Jones did by renaming the Gazos Creek access road a "fire trail" in order to get state support. When the State had empty pockets, pressure was applied on the three counties surrounding Big Basin to provide money for efforts like saving the Butano forest. When this failed, personal connections sometimes worked, as with the gifts of land from Middleton, Bloom, Hartman and the McAbee family — all Club members or supporters.

The Sempervirens Club did not engage in raising funds from individuals and businesses in order to purchase land from private owners that contained endangered redwoods. They may have chosen that tactic because the Save-the-Redwoods League, with whom Club presidents had been in continuous contact since 1918, was already tapping that source with considerable success. Tens of thousands of acres of redwoods in northern California had been preserved in state and national parks through the League's fundraising efforts. In 1967, in conjunction with the Sierra Club, the League had secured funds to purchase 488 acres of redwoods in the Berry Creek area from the Big Creek Lumber Company for inclusion in Big Basin Redwoods State Park, permanently preventing logging within sight of the scenic falls. While the Sempervirens Club provided support, it remained in the background. Club President Herbert Jones was in his 80's and had retired from the public eye with his law practice, and many of the other Club activists were deceased or quite elderly.

The Sempervirens Club retained its position as a pioneer in the preservation movement though. In a 1992 article on land trusts, the *Sierra Club Magazine* included the Sempervirens Club among the trailblazers in this movement. Land trusts today are nonprofit organizations that work to preserve land threatened by commercial development, from logging to suburban sprawl. In many cases, they function as mediators between private owners and public agencies, buying land and reselling it to public agencies for county, regional, state or federal parks. The Save-the-Redwoods League had pioneered this particular approach in California. By the late 1950's, The Nature Conservancy, modeled after a quasi-governmental organization of the same name in Britain, was purchasing land on a national level, and the Greenbelt Alliance was preserving land in the San Francisco Bay Area. In 1963, writer Wallace Stegner formed the Committee for Green Foothills to lobby for preservation of open space in San Mateo and Santa Clara counties. The tremendous growth in population after World War II had stimulated a construction and development boom in the nine counties surrounding the San Francisco Bay. A successful state park bond issue in 1964 made funds available for park expansion. Since private contributions could be matched with state funds from the bond act, a doubling effect occurred with individual donations. Thus the means and the desire — as represented by the bond act and by individual donations — to increase public ownership of undeveloped land all came together at a propitious time. It was the dawning of the national environmental movement in the mid-1960's.

By 1968, Big Basin Redwoods State Park was receiving high public use. More than 7,000 campers had been turned away the previous year for lack of room. At the same time, the area was being threatened with severe ecological damage from logging and development on over 750 acres of private land in key locations within the boundaries of the watershed. There were plans for a hotel-resort complex on a 2,300 acre parcel between the park and the coast. Another land

developer in north Santa Cruz County, was planning a subdivision on more than 300 acres on the side of Mt. McAbee in the heart of Big Basin. Edgar Weyburn, President of the Sierra Club, had previously asked Claude A. "Tony" Look, Chairman of the Sierra Club's National Conservation Committee, to work with John Dewitt of the Save-the-Redwoods League on the Berry Creek purchase; $24,000 had been

Claude A. "Tony" Look
*Photo: C. R. Boothe, Private Collection*

raised, with the State matching those funds. Then Look was asked to find an additional $19,000 to combine with $108,000 available from the League and the State to purchase the Mt. McAbee acreage. But he had only one month in which to do it. Tony Look's "May Day" campaign was short, intense and successful. In fact, the ad hoc committee he organized raised more than enough for the Mt. McAbee purchase and was able to secure additional land.

Big Basin was similar to the Bull Creek basin, a 25,000 acre area in Humboldt County where Tony Look's father and paternal grandfather, had a ranch at Look's Prairie in the Bull Creek drainage. His father operated a restaurant in Garberville in addition to propagating irises. His grandfather had been a logger for Pacific Lumber Company and worked a two-ended saw six days a week. "We'll never run out of redwoods", he told his grandson who fished for salmon, steelhead and trout in the Eel River and liked to hike along Sproul Creek. Look had also met the founders of the Save-the-Redwoods League and had accompanied them on an exploration of fossil shells along the South Fork of the Eel River. After receiving degrees in pharmacy and pharmaceutical chemistry from UC Berkeley, Look settled in the Bay Area with his family. He joined the Sierra Club in 1940 to ski at their Sierra lodge near Donner Pass to pursue his interest in trails. After service in World War II, Look returned home for a visit. He found that the banks of Sproul Creek had been stripped and the fishing ruined. Heavy flood waters in Humboldt County in 1955, made worse by the deforestation, eventually destroyed all evidence of the Look family burial plot in the town where his father was raised. Meanwhile, Look had moved with his family to Los Altos in the 1950's and he owned and operated the Monta Vista Drug Store in Cupertino. At the time he joined the Loma Prieta Chapter of the Sierra Club, it had become involved in zoning issues in Santa Clara County. San Jose was expanding its borders westward to include new property developments. Although the County Planning Director was conservation-minded and the county had established greenways along all the creeks, much agricultural land was being turned into housing developments.

In 1999, Look related that, "I guess I learned to love the redwoods when I was a boy. I saw what happened when they bought trees for a park, but not the watershed. Logging and fires caused erosion below and trees started falling. Then I saw that the same thing was happening in the Sierra foothills and I saw that development was beginning in the Santa Cruz Mountains and the same thing could happen". He took science classes at San Jose State College in order to understand more about ecology. Working with the Sierra Club's Conservation Committee, he helped stop the Grand Canal portion of the California aqueduct which would have tunneled under the forest in Mendocino, and prevented a dam on the Eel River which would have flooded much of the Round Valley Indian Reservation. At a friend's photography store in Mountain View, Look met Howard King and they began a long friendship and a partnership on behalf of the Santa Cruz redwoods. After retiring as an engineer for Hewlett Packard, King had been told by his doctor that walking would help his bad back. He went into Big Basin with a camera in 1959, and began what would become life-long photography and trail blazing in the park. His photographs of redwoods and their surroundings have been widely published and used for promotion materials by the Sempervirens Fund,

Sierra Club, and the Save-the-Redwoods League. A trail in Big Basin was named after him and both he and Look were made honorary rangers by the California State Park Rangers Association, for their efforts on behalf of State Parks.

Despite the Berry Creek and May Day fundraising successes, Big Basin would remain both endangered and incomplete. In the summer of 1968, Look and King joined forces with another organization, Conservation Associates, to find a means to protect the entire Waddell Creek

The Castle Rock at Castle Rock State Park.
*Photo: Alexander Lowry, Sempervirens Fund Collection*

watershed as well as to establish a new state park fourteen miles northeast of Big Basin. Conservation Associates had been formed in 1960 by three environmental activists: Doris Leonard, who with her husband Richard, had been a longtime conservationist in the Sierra Club; George Collins, recently retired as Chief of Land Use Planning with the Western Region of the National Park Service; and Dorothy Varian, the widow of Silicon Valley electronics pioneer Russell Varian, inventor of the Klystron tube and founder of Varian Associates. Varian had hiked the Santa Cruz Mountains extensively

Founders Grove, Big Basin Redwoods State Park.

*Photo: Alexander Lowry, Sempervirens Fund Collection*

in his youth and was particularly fond of Castle Rock. On the crest of a 3,200 foot ridge, the area offers a labyrinthine outcrop of Chico sandstone where rock climbers practiced and kids explored the honey-combed aeolian caves. In 1959, Russell Varian had obtained an option to buy twenty-six acres in the Castle Rock area from Ione Welch, daughter of Judge James Welch, an early Director of the Sempervirens Club. A week after the option was secured, Varian died while on a hiking trip in Alaska with the Leonards. The families, who shared business dealings as well as a love for hiking, decided to fulfill Varian's vision of preserving a

representative cross section of the mountains as a memorial to him. Conservation Associates was used as the vehicle to achieve this. During the 1960's, the group was also involved in preserving the Nipomo Dunes in San Luis Obispo County; the Point Reyes Seashore, which would become a National Park; Andrew Molera State Park in the Big Sur area; and 10,000 acres in Santa Cruz County which in 1963 became the Forest of Nisene Marks State Park.

According to Richard Leonard, who had also been President of both the Sierra Club and Save-the-Redwoods League, Conservation Associates "revived the old Sempervirens Club of 1900, which was the sparkplug for the Big Basin Redwoods State Park. It had an excellent name and history, and it was a legal corporation. So I suggested, through the Conservation Law Society, that we revive the corporation, change the name from Sempervirens Club to Sempervirens Fund, to reflect a new emphasis and continue". The new organization was to be called Sempervirens Fund of Conservation Associates. It met for the first time on June 24, 1968, at Dorothy Varian's home in Cupertino. Tony Look, Howard King, Dorothy Varian, Doris Leonard, and George Collins formed the nucleus. The group also included fund raising consultant Allen Jamieson; Sierra Club activist Phillipa Pfeiffer; and Walter Ward, General Manager of Vallco Shopping Center and a movie producer for the Sierra Club. Walter Hays, an attorney for the new Sempervirens Fund, brought Herbert Jones' blessing along with the articles of incorporation for the Sempervirens Club. The objectives of the new organization were to "complete" both Big Basin and Castle Rock, which had just been designated as a state park. The goal was to more than double the size of both parks, and to connect them with a trail along the Saratoga Gap road over the right-of-way obtained by Andrew Hill fifty-five years before. In addition, the new group wanted to develop a trail system linking Big Basin and Castle Rock with Portola and Butano State Parks in San Mateo County and with county parks in Santa Clara and San Mateo counties. Although the Fund organizers may have been unaware at the time of the "great park" envisioned at the turn of the century by the founders of the Sempervirens Club, they were moving decisively in that direction.

The Sempervirens Fund of Conservation Associates established an address at Stanford University and a list of sponsors that included Ansel Adams, Newton Drury, State Parks Director William Penn Mott, Jr., chemist Carl Djerassi, and David Packard. Also included were former Sempervirens Club directors Herbert Jones, Samuel Leask, and Clyde Arbuckle. A five-year campaign to raise $3.5 million, with $1.75 million from public contributions and memberships began with a ceremony to erect a bronze plaque at Slippery Rock in Big Basin where the Sempervirens Club had been founded on May 18, 1900. The funds were to be used to purchase over 700 acres of inholdings in Big Basin and additional land for Castle Rock. This event was followed by a kickoff for the general public in October at the Santa Clara County fairgrounds which featured a dinner and guest speakers. William Penn Mott, Jr. was there to formally receive the deed for the Mt. McAbee purchase and the transfer of Castle Rock land to the State. The new organization was also announced in an issue of the *Sierra Club Bulletin* which headlined its plans "to complete and connect California's oldest and newest state parks". Written by Allen Jamieson, the article featured a color photo by King of Berry Creek Falls.

The offices of the Sempervirens Fund were in the back of Look's Cupertino pharmacy until more suitable offices could be secured in Los Altos. George Collins reluctantly served as President for the next four years until the Fund could receive its own non-profit, tax deductible status and separate from Conservation Associates. Los Altos physician Richard Wheat, who had been a scoutmaster with Look, became President in 1972 and served in that role for fifteen years. Dr. Wheat's father, Attorney Carl Wheat, a noted historian, map maker and author, had been an advisor for Olmsted's park survey in the 1920's. Unlike the earlier movement though, most of the initial membership and financial support for the Sempervirens Fund came from individuals in San Mateo County rather than from the San Jose or Santa Cruz areas where the Club's support had been. Much as Andrew Hill had taken a leadership role in the Club, Tony Look undertook that function in the new Fund. He took a course in grantsmanship. A mailing list was developed to support solicitations, and the organization gradually became more professional.

Direction for the Sempervirens Fund's involvement in the improvement of park infrastructure, came when State Parks trails engineer Dale Wilson located the deeds for the right-of-way originally obtained by Andrew Hill. In April 1969, more than 2,500 people participated in a two-day project to construct the "Skyline-to-the-Sea Trail" from Castle Rock to Big Basin. This event was co-sponsored by the Santa Cruz Mountains Trails Association and has been held yearly since then. Trail Days became a national event in 1994 with the promotion of National Trail Days under the sponsorship of the American Hiking Society with several thousand people involved in creating and improving trails in parks across the country.

Waddell Beach, Rancho del Oso and Big Basin beyond.
*Photo: Alexander Lowry, Sempervirens Fund Collection*

In the early 1970's, State Parks Director William Penn Mott, Jr. formally defined the boundaries of the park for the Fund and prioritized a list of twelve parcels in Big Basin that the Department wanted to acquire in order to protect the Waddell Creek watershed. The highest priority on Mott's list was the 2,300-acre Hoover ranch located in the valley where Waddell Creek empties into the Pacific Ocean. President Herbert Hoover's brother Theodore first saw the land during a geology trip in 1898 while an engineering student at Stanford University. He bought the property fifteen years later from the owners of the Ocean Shore Railroad, which was bankrupt after the 1906 earthquake, and the heirs of William Waddell. Hoover named his property Rancho del Oso, "Ranch of the Bear". He moved there with his wife and three daughters in March, 1914. According to one of his daughters, Hulda Hoover McLean:

*That first day was pure magic. I stood still in the field in front of the new house and was absorbed into the spell of the valley — fragrance of earth and flowers, color and motion of butterflies, clouds, rippling grass and dancing trees. Its music — song of birds, distant surf, wind in the forest — sang itself into my heart.*

The ranch ran five miles up the Waddell and was about three-fourths of a mile wide, with open meadows in the lowlands and 800 foot high wooded ridges. Shortly before the 1971 Christmas holiday season, developers had offered the Hoover family $2,000 an acre for the land and had plans for a 2,000 acre resort hotel complex, including an airport, golf course, and lake. The Sempervirens Fund sprang into action, soliciting donations as Christmas gifts to purchase the ranch. Recipients of these donation-gifts received a simulated decorative deed suitable for framing. The next year, the State appropriated $2.5 million through special legislation to buy the Hoover land, but the owners backed away from the offer when they felt they could not negotiate the long-term occupancy they wanted. It would be several years until the details of occupancy were resolved and Rancho del Oso was added to Big Basin Redwoods State Park.

The Fund was successful in the purchase of a 155 acre ridge along the north rim of Big Basin containing one of the last remaining stands of primeval redwoods. The parcel valued at $825,000 was owned by the Locatelli family, a Santa Cruz Mountains dynasty prominent in logging. The family donated $180,000 of the purchase price as a gift to the State, and the remaining donations came from the following: Save-the-Redwoods

League ($250,000), Sempervirens Fund ($83,050) and Federal Land and Water Conservation Fund ($311,950). The Save-the-Redwoods League, with the assistance of Sempervirens Fund, was also able to buy 320 acres of land scheduled to be logged by the Santa Cruz Lumber Company. Again, in combination with the Save-the-Redwoods League, another 260 acres were purchased from the Anderson and Seechrist families. The first purchases of land in Castle Rock included properties owned by the Wallace, Clement-Hays, and Jordan families. Not everyone however, was in favor of increasing the size of the parks in the Santa Cruz Mountains. Hearings to review the parkland expansion were held by the Santa Cruz County Board of Supervisors and, according to one newspaper account, the State's plans "got a decidedly chilly response". Supervisor Tom Black was "totally against the state getting more property. They just come in, acquire it, and then don't develop it, use it, lease it, or do a thing with it. And it's off the tax rolls. I can't support this". The county also wanted the State to pay an "in-lieu" tax to repay the county for property taxes lost on the state parks. A rumored closure of Highway 236 through the park in order to control visitors, and the possibility of access from the coast through the Theodore Hoover property, upset business owners in the San Lorenzo Valley who worried about losing tourist traffic. Residents in the rugged Last Chance Road area on the southern border of the park obtained a map purportedly showing the properties the State wanted to purchase in the area which caused concern and objections from local owners. An official of the State Department of Parks and Recreation told a meeting of nearly one hundred angry Last Chance Road land owners that "we're not buying the park for one person, you know, we're buying it for 20 million Californians". Although the state had raised nearly $1.25 million to purchase up to 1,500 acres, or seventy-nine private parcels, a buying spree did not occur. Only 136 acres at the junction of Last Chance Creek and the east fork of the Waddell were purchased at that time.

Tony Look and Howard King had been involved with spring planting of trees for the Sierra Club, and they continued the practice in Big Basin. The reforestation project, similar to the one Club President Wallace Isham had

contemplated in the 1920's, became a profitable fund-raiser for the Fund, with sponsorship of newly-planted trees for a five, ten, or twenty-dollar donation. The planted tree program was successful in persuading civic groups such as the Soroptomists to plant trees. Look and King got the idea of providing trees as memorials in exchange for a contribution from a church-centered solicitation project in Africa. The first memorial grove of California redwoods — the Bolling Grove in Humboldt County — had been dedicated in 1921 by the Save-the-Redwoods League to the first officer to fall in World War I. The Sempervirens Fund began to offer standing trees — redwoods in Big Basin and madrones or oaks in Castle Rock — in groves or individually, as memorial tributes or as gifts for special occasions. Campsites in both parks could also be named for donors to the Fund.

Sempervirens Fund efforts were not limited to trail building and fund raising. In the early 1970's, the Sempervirens Fund sponsored two field studies in the Santa Cruz Mountains. A team of professors, undergraduate, and graduate students in biology from San Jose State University conducted a two-part study of Castle Rock State Park, taking a natural resources inventory and preparing an environmental impact report to help distinguish areas for trails and camping from land that should be left in a natural state. Students in the Environmental Studies Department at the University of California at Santa Cruz examined the entire Waddell Creek watershed and published a lengthy report detailing geologic, hydrologic, and biologic processes in the ecosystem. "Acquisition of the entire watershed is a complex and lengthy process", noted the report writers, "involving well over 100 owners, numerous settlers, and other users of the natural resources, private and public organizations, and more than a dozen governmental bodies". The report suggested that the first priorities for state park expansion should include the purchase of the larger, private holdings before they were subdivided.

A major impetus was given to redwood forest watershed preservation with the accidental discovery of the nest of the marbled murrelet in Big Basin Redwoods State Park. The marbled murrelet had been the only remaining North American breeding bird whose nest had not been found. In 1974, a tree trimmer was removing potentially dangerous limbs from a two hundred foot tall tree in one of Big Basin's campgrounds. Out of that tree fell an immature marbled murrelet. A threatened species, the murrelet was now known to nest in California's coast redwood forests, and protecting one protects the other. That logic has prevailed not only in Big Basin but in other redwood regions as well. It is not without irony that the marbled murrelet's nest was discovered in California's first state park on the original acquisition made possible by the Sempervirens Club in 1902, and was identified by State Park Ranger Denzil Verardo who was also a Sempervirens Fund member. Succeeding preservation efforts by the Sempervirens Club and Fund had protected not only the coast redwoods of the Santa Cruz Mountains, but also the critical habitat of the threatened marbled murrelet.

Rock formation at Castle Rock State Park.
*Photo: Alexander Lowry, Sempervirens Fund Collection*

In 1976, the State finally concluded negotiations with Theodore Hoover's heirs to purchase almost 1,600 acres of Rancho del Oso for inclusion in Big Basin. This enabled the "Skyline-to-the-Sea Trail" to be extended thirty-five miles from Castle Rock to the Pacific Ocean. In Castle Rock State Park, the Sempervirens Fund secured several key parcels. The gift of twenty-five acres from Paul Chesebrough was coupled with the purchase of an adjoining parcel at "Sempervirens Point" to effectively block a planned subdivision. Chesebrough had inherited thousands of acres from his aunt, Edith Van Ardsdale, who had been a strong supporter of the Fund's objectives. Also added to the park were MacDonald Ridge (160 acres) and Fat Buck Ridge (forty-four acres) above Deer Creek, along with the Hull-Farman property (twelve and one-half acres). Proposition 1, the 1974 park bond that had provided matching funds for these purchases, also provided $3 million towards land acquisition in Big Basin and Castle Rock, and $400,000 for land for trails in the Santa Cruz Mountains.

In 1977, in its most ambitious project to date, the Sempervirens Fund optioned the 730 acre Mountain Shadows Ranch between Castle Rock and Highway 9, a critical acquisition which would increase the size of Castle Rock State Park by fifty percent. An emergency fund drive was done to raise the down payment. Tom Harris, an environmental reporter for the *San Jose Mercury*, termed the purchase "the gamble at Saratoga Gap", since it could tie up money

that might be needed for other land threatened by development. The densely-wooded property, which included gently-rolling hills and meadows and steep slopes and canyons, was purchased two years later as the Fund raised nearly $240,000 in donations to pay its share of the purchase price.

In its Annual Report celebrating ten years of preservation efforts, the Sempervirens Fund announced that it had added 1,376 acres to Big Basin Redwoods State Park, and 1,131 acres to Castle Rock State Park, which was then near completion. In addition to land acquisition, volunteers in Fund programs had planted 11,600 trees in the parks and helped build seventy miles of new trails along with reconstructing old paths. On "Clean-up Day", hundreds of volunteers from school groups, scouting programs, and civic organizations combed the parks to find and remove litter. Numerous standing trees, redwood groves, and campsites were dedicated in the two parks. More than $360,000 had been raised in contributions that year by the Sempervirens Fund and the organization had secured nearly $260,000 in matching funds from the State. On May 6, 1977, the 50th anniversary of California's State Park System and the 10th anniversary of Sempervirens Fund were celebrated at Big Basin in the pageant, "Slippery Rock Gang". Fund members and descendants of Club members were featured in the roles of the 1900-era founders. Howard King, the Sempervirens Fund photographer, played Andrew Hill, the Sempervirens Club photographer.

In 1979, the Sempervirens Fund launched an ambitious two-year "Today for Tomorrow" campaign to raise $516,000 to acquire over 500 acres in Big Basin and Castle Rock, and along the "Skyline-to-the-Sea Trail". According to Fund President Dr. Richard Wheat, land purchased with this money would help join the parks together. "The geographical locations of these parks, so near the great metropolitan Bay Area, makes them available to millions in spite of our shrinking energy resources. People can and will come to these areas to replenish their needs for the 'natural experience' so missing in our urban sprawl". Included in the campaign purchase was the 100 acre Summit Meadows adjacent to Mountain Shadows Ranch, which offered spectacular vistas of the surrounding countryside.

The energy crisis of the mid-1970's and tightening Federal fiscal policies reduced resources to facilitate park preservation efforts. The 1978 passage of Proposition 13 signaled a California taxpayers' revolt that would further reduce the amount of state and local funds available for park support. The Sempervirens Fund was forced to redouble its efforts to convince donors that investing in land today would reap tenfold benefits in the future.

In the early 1980's, a former Christmas tree farm and an orchard were added to Castle Rock, and the owners of the historic 125 acre Trays Ranch on the northern border of Big Basin deeded a half-interest in their property to the Fund. Visitors who traveled to Big Basin by horseback in the early years from Palo Alto had stayed overnight at Trays Ranch which was the site of springs forming the headwaters for Boulder Creek, Little Boulder Creek, and a tributary of Opal Creek. The Fund purchased the Hollow Tree Mill property (eighty-nine acres) along China Grade. The seventy-nine acre Eagle Rock parcel, which includes a sandstone outcropping with 360-degree views of Big Basin and the Santa Cruz Mountains and with some of the last rare and endangered Santa Cruz cypress trees, was added to Big Basin State Park. The Fund was also able to prevent logging by buying several properties along Blooms Creek on the southern border of Big Basin State Park. It purchased the 298 acre Hickory Oak Ridge, which presented opportunities for trails linking Castle Rock and

Big Basin with the Midpeninsula Regional Open Space District's Long Ridge Preserve and Portola State Park.

By 1985, Tony Look had decided to retire. As co-founder and Executive Director of the Sempervirens Fund for seventeen years, the organization had achieved most of the objectives agreed to with State Parks Director Mott in 1968. There were 14,000 potential contributors on the donor mailing list. Look had been able to raise up to $800,000 a year. But more would be needed to achieve new Fund goals, and Tony Look felt he had reached his professional level as a fundraiser. Verlyn Clausen was hired as the new Executive Director and Look remained on the Sempervirens Fund Board of Directors and served in a new capacity, as Director of Land Affairs.

"I'm enamored with the natural state of anything", Look recounted explaining his many years of preservation work in the Santa Cruz Mountains. "While most people just want a place where nature can do its thing", he observed, "I do this so that if you came back in a thousand years, you could see the natural succession here. That gives me a feeling that time, trees, bugs, and all things are connected. It's about the closest we can come to grasping the meaning of eternity or being ageless ourselves."

The Sempervirens Fund was able to achieve its goals because "we caught a wave of the environmental movement, but the later years are not as romantic as the early years", Look continued. The task now was to expand campaigns for specific properties. Other land conservancy groups such as, the Peninsula Open Space Trust and Midpeninsula Regional Open Space District, had joined with the Sempervirens Fund to stop urban sprawl and the development of second home sites in the Santa Cruz Mountains. "Now we have a vision of connecting parks", Look explained. The next phase of the Sempervirens Fund's work would be to target land in Butano and Pescadero as well as Big Basin and Castle Rock and to develop trail corridors between them. The "greater park" of 45,000 to 60,000 acres in the Santa Cruz Mountains that was envisioned by the founders of the Sempervirens Club in the early 1900's began to take shape in the combination of county, regional, and state parks.

Sempervirens members restage the 1904 photo in 1975.    *Photo: Sempervirens Fund Collection*

# IX.

## New Leadership — New Challenges

*Watershed protection is the only way to assure long-term protection of parks in state lands, and the integrity of an ecological system.*

**Verlyn Clausen, Executive Director of the Sempervirens Fund, 1999**

By the time that Verlyn Clausen, a former land planning consultant and Lutheran pastor, became Executive Director of the Sempervirens Fund, in1985, it had become increasingly difficult to preserve land in the Santa Cruz Mountains. An exploding population in the nearby inland valleys encouraged housing developers to push up into the foothills and even to the mountain tops. Conservative administrations in Sacramento and Washington had become reluctant to offer government aid for public land purchases. After years of preservation support at the polls, voters began defeating propositions to fund parks. Clausen was faced with difficult challenges and made use of a variety of tools developed by land trusts to expand the borders of Castle Rock and Big Basin, and to connect these parks with Portola, Butano and Año Nuevo State Parks.

Nationally, the land trust movement had grown alongside the environmental movement. The Land Trust Alliance, a national membership organization of land trusts founded in 1982, described these organizations working hand-in-hand with landowners using a variety of tools. Tools such as conservation easements that permanently restrict the uses of the land, land donations and purchases, and strategic estate planning, to protect America's open spaces and green places, increasingly threatened by sprawl and development. Local, regional and national lands trusts, often staffed by volunteers or just a few employees, are helping communities save America's land heritage without relying exclusively on the deep pockets of government.

While some land trusts manage the land they receive, the Sempervirens Fund, like the Save-the-Redwoods League, holds it only temporarily until it can be transferred to an agency like the California State Department of Parks and Recreation. County and regional park organizations have also been formed to manage public land. In 1933, the California Legislature had passed the Regional Park District Act enabling the formation of park districts within the boundaries of existing utility districts and including more than a single county. The model for this form of land management was the East Bay Regional Park District which was organized the following year with its acquisition of Tilden Regional Park. In 1972, voters in northwestern Santa Clara County approved an initiative creating the Midpeninsula Regional Park District, which has since been renamed the Midpeninsula Regional Open Space District (MROSD). Two years later, voters in southern San Mateo County joined the district, and in 1992 a small portion of Santa Cruz County was annexed by the district. The Peninsula Open Space Trust (POST) was formed in 1977 to work primarily with the district in acquiring land, similar to the arrangement between the Fund and State Parks. In 1976, the California Coastal Conservancy was created. A unique state agency, the Conservancy was established to assist local governments and other public agencies, nonprofit groups, and private landowners in protecting and preserving coastal properties.

According to the Land Trust Alliance, a recent census of land trusts nationwide identified 1,213 organizations which have protected approximately 4.7 million acres of land. It soon became apparent to the Sempervirens Fund, that it could benefit from working together with other organizations to pursue its objectives, which Clausen had assisted in formally defining in 1986:

*(The Sempervirens Fund will) work to preserve and protect the natural character of California's Santa Cruz Mountains and to encourage appropriate public enjoyment of this environment. We seek to achieve this by acquiring suitable land in a working partnership with the State of California and other public and private agencies, by completing Big Basin Redwoods and Castle Rock State Parks, by fostering public participation in activities such as reforestation and trail projects, and by linking parks and open spaces to provide an integrated park land system.*

Cooperation with all of these organizations — along with new fund-raising and land-acquisition tools and techniques, and federal legislation which recognized conservation easements as tax-deductible contributions — became critical as the Sempervirens Fund worked to achieve its goals during this time of government fiscal belt-tightening.

New Fund Executive Director Verlyn Clausen had been raised in Nebraska and "always felt

Waddell Beach and Rancho del Oso.
*Photo: Alexander Lowry, Sempervirens Fund Collection*

constrained by heavy urbanization. It feels right to have open space around me". He saw that open space was becoming rare "as urbanization fills the Santa Clara — now Silicon — Valley, and moves out toward the forested slopes of the mountains and the ocean beyond". The challenge as Clausen saw it, was "that we complete the ecological system of the two parks as quickly as possible", as well as establish a trail system that would tie the parks together and include other public spaces in the Santa Cruz Mountains. While increasing the participation of individual donors, Clausen vigorously pursued foundations and corporations for contributions. Combining with acquisitions in San Mateo County by Peninsula Open Space Trust, the Midpeninsula Regional Open Space District, and the Trust for Public Lands, the Sempervirens Fund under Clausen's leadership, continued the work of constructing the "greater park" that had been envisioned by Sempervirens Club's founders more than eighty years earlier.

In the mid-1980's, the Sempervirens Fund began a series of coordinated campaigns that targeted more than one desired property. The first, "Mountains & the Sea", was conducted in two stages. In "Phase I – The Mountains" - the goal was acquisition of Craig Springs Canyon, 100 acres at the headwaters of the San Lorenzo River. Surrounded by Castle Rock parkland it featured redwoods and ferns as well as rocky outcroppings and grassy meadows. With matching funds from the State and contributions from the Sierra Club Foundation and the Packard Foundation, the Fund obtained the $175,000 needed for purchase. "Phase II – The Sea" - raised nearly $300,000 to purchase the Pacific View Ranch from the heirs of Theodore Hoover. Fifty acres originally purchased by the family in 1914, adjoins Highway One and the Rancho del Oso portion of Big Basin park to which it was added. The family ranch home was converted into the Rancho del Oso Nature and History Center. Assistance in the purchase of that property was provided by a loan from the Coastal Conservancy and by contributions from the Hearst Foundation and the Berkeley-based Strong Center for Environmental Values.

In 1987, the 60th anniversary of the 1927 founding of the state park system was celebrated with a "Homecoming" event in Big Basin attended by over three hundred guests. Tony Look and Howard King were honored for their efforts on behalf of California's parks. At the annual dinner of the Founders Club of the Sempervirens Fund, for donors who have contributed $500 or more to fund-raising campaigns, California Department of Parks and Recreation Chief Planner Ross Henry spoke to members about the importance of preserving parks adjacent to metropolitan centers to serve inner-city residents. He promised his agency's support of the Sempervirens Fund goal of completing Big Basin and Castle Rock State Parks. In that propitious year, an Interpretive Center, built at a cost of $71,000, was dedicated in Castle Rock; the $36,000 Cañon del Oso bridge over the lower Waddell was completed. Other events included a 10K race on Big Basin's trails which, under stormy skies, drew 340 runners. The Fund began an annual Leaders in Conservation Awards Dinner, which in its inaugural year honored Artemas and Edward Ginzton. The 1987 honoree would be Dorothy Varian, who had a Land Reserve Fund established in her name for Castle Rock State Park. The Fund was started by a $100,000 matching fund grant from the Save-the-Redwoods League, Conservation Associates and William Hewlett.

Most of the large parcels under private ownership in both Castle Rock and Big Basin Redwoods State Park, had been purchased by the late 1980's. The Sempervirens Fund now had the added challenge of finding new acquisition opportunities as well as facing the hurdles posed by decreasing government assistance. "We have continually tried to seize unexpected opportunities, arising with increasing frequency, to acquire critical parcels within the short period of time they are available," Clausen announced to supporters in *The Mountain Echo*, the quarterly newsletter the Fund named after W.S. Rodgers' *Boulder Creek Mountain Echo*. Clausen articulated his concept of "critical parcels opportunity purchasing", and said the Fund would make use of loans from sympathetic conservation groups and individuals in order to secure threatened property that required immediate action, even if "we occasionally push our resources to the limit in order to obtain them". He distinguished "critical parcels" which require quick funding from planned acquisitions which resulted from discussions with State Park officials concerning long-range priorities in the Santa Cruz Mountains.

"Mountains & the Sea", was followed by the two-year, "Road to the Redwoods" campaign beginning in 1987. The goal was the purchase of a group of properties on the edge of Big Basin — a total of nearly 200 acres with a price tag of over $500,000. Some of the land had been developed and was in need of reforestation. Matching funds were expected from the State. The properties at Big Basin's "front door" along Highway 236 were prime candidates for development if the Sempervirens Fund had not successfully acquired them for the park. At the completion of the "Road to the Redwoods" campaign, a brass plaque with the names of 270 major donors was erected by the Fund at the entrance to the park as a visible "thank you".

1988 was the 20th anniversary of the establishment of the Sempervirens Fund. Tony Look was honored as the third recipient of the Leaders in Conservation Award for his dedication and leadership, resulting in the addition of more than 5,000 acres to Big Basin and Castle Rock, as well as the initiation of the annual Trail Days and park reforestation projects. Over 23,000 trees had been planted, and more than sixty miles of trails had been built and maintained. The Sempervirens Fund joined with other environmental groups and the representatives from university, corporate, and governmental communities at a conference in Berkeley on "Restoring the Earth". A book of the same name was published by author John Berger featuring a chapter on Tony Look and his work in conservation. During this period, California voters overwhelmingly endorsed Proposition 70 to restore mountain lion habitat which would provide $2 million to help purchase land in Big Basin and Castle Rock.

The Sempervirens Fund began its third decade with its third major campaign. This time the Fund needed to raise $1.4 million for 809 acres on Berry Creek Ridge. With a loan from the David and Lucille Packard Foundation to cover the down payment and nearly $1 million expected from Proposition 70 money, it was the largest and most ambitious project yet undertaken. The property was owned by Sequoia Forest Industries in Idaho. The company was headed by Ron Yanke who also owned the coastal Gray Whale Ranch in Santa Cruz County. The Berry Creek Ridge property included the headwaters of Berry and Waddell Creeks at the northwest corner of the park. It contained scattered stands of old-growth redwoods even though the ridge, as part of the Hanna Tree Farm, had been logged continuously since the late 1800's. It was a critical section of the watershed to protect, and its purchase would guarantee that protection. Substantial support came from the Bryan family who contributed $100,000 to the campaign in honor of former Sempervirens Fund Board member Everett Bryan. After the final payment was made a year later and the land turned over to the state, a trail was constructed through the property and a marker erected containing the names of those donating $1,000 or more to the project.

Palo Alto Assemblymember, now State Senator, Byron Sher was the honoree at the fourth annual Leaders in Conservation Dinner. Retired National Park Service Director William Penn Mott, Jr. presented the award and the keynote address was given by Martin Rosen, President of the Trust for Public Land. Rosen praised the Sempervirens Fund for being a "savvy, experienced, and universally respected organization". At the annual Founders Club Dinner, the Honorable L. William (Bill) Lane, publisher of *Sunset* magazine and former U.S. Ambassador to Australia, said that the Fund has "been in the forefront...one of the most successful in achieving goals that no one conceived might have been obtained through a private, volunteer group". The Sempervirens Fund helped organize the Bay Area Ridge Trail Project to establish a 400-mile trail through counties around the Bay, that had first been envisioned by Mott. Efforts went beyond the pick and shovel as the Fund co-produced a twenty-seven minute interpretive documentary with the State of California entitled, "On the Edge: Nature's Last Stand for Coast Redwoods". The video, written by San Jose State University graduate student Jim Snyder, focused on the natural history of the coast redwood from prehistoric times to the present day. It featured interviews with Clausen, Look, Mott, and John Dewitt, Executive Director of the Save-the-Redwoods League.

The 90th anniversary of the Sempervirens Club was marked with a slightly soggy celebration in Big Basin where about 100 revelers listened to "The Birth of Big Basin", a skit in rhyme written by park docent June Bauman.

Although the focus of the Sempervirens Fund had been on land acquisition in Big Basin during the early years of the 1990's, additional properties were targeted in Castle Rock as well.

One parcel was Toll Road Woods, a rugged and beautiful forty-six acre landscape surrounded on three sides by the park and on the fourth by Highway 9. Passing through the property, in addition to the "Skyline-to-the-Sea Trail", is the historic Saratoga Toll Road Trail which was built in the late 1860's as a way to move cordwood to San Jose. In addition to State matching funds toward the $267,200 cost and assistance from the Packard, Varian, and Roberts Foundations, the culminating gift was made by the Hearst Corporation's *Countryside* magazine. The next purchase was a neighboring property, Tin Can Ranch. Settled in the 1860's by two families, the thirty-nine acre ranch was logged at the turn of the century and, according to local legend, the loggers lived off of canned food and tossed the empty cans onto a heap outside their cabins — hence the name. Once again, the Sempervirens Fund was able to draw upon a wide variety of financial partners to raise the $648,000 needed to purchase this important addition to Castle Rock. Restoration on a 250 acre parcel in Castle Rock purchased by the state almost a decade earlier was also begun. It contained the only remaining Black Oak forest in Santa Cruz County, and had been partially cleared for an orchard in the 1880's. In 1957, a seventy acre section had been converted to a Christmas tree farm and 70,000 fir trees planted. All were removed in the restoration.

"I continue to be amazed at the pressure to develop the Santa Cruz Mountains", Clausen told an interviewer in the *San Jose Mercury News*. "We feel a real urgency in what we're doing." The reporter noted that as middlemen the non-profit conservancies reduce the state's cost of buying park land, thus allowing more wilderness and open space to be preserved. Because of the tax incentives they provide, they can buy land cheaper than developers...without the burden of bureaucracy, conservancies such as Sempervirens are able to acquire land much faster than the state can.

But while State matching funds were available in the short-term for Fund projects, the defeat of environmental initiatives in the early 1990's left the Fund with no supplemental resources for preservation efforts. Building up the land reserve fund, Clausen stated, "is the only way to truly ensure that we can respond effectively whenever the opportunity to purchase endangered lands occur". Other sources helped. The

Patagonia clothing firm awarded the Fund $2,000 through its Environmental Tithing Program and an $11,000 challenge grant came from the Dean Witter Foundation for the Fund's restoration efforts.

Tom and Susie McCarthy received the fifth Leaders in Conservation Award. Tom McCarthy, a Director of the Sempervirens Fund from 1977 to 1991, was Vice-President and General Counsel for Kaiser Aluminum and had been honored by the Nature Conservancy for protecting Elkhorn Slough in Monterey County. Speaking at the awards luncheon was Brian O'Neill, General Manager of the 73,000 acre Golden Gate National Recreation Area — the largest urban National Park. Conservation biologist Michael Soulé of the University of California at Santa Cruz was guest speaker at the Founders Club Dinner that year. Continuing a Club tradition of honoring supporters with trees, a memorial grove was dedicated in Big Basin by the extended Wing Family and by the California State Park Rangers Association, to the memory of Colonel Charles B. Wing, who played such a significant role in the preservation efforts in Big Basin.

In the summer of 1991, the Sempervirens Fund assisted the Midpeninsula Regional Open Space District by selling it the 116 acre Hickory Oak Ridge property at Saratoga Gap, at the intersection of Highways 9 and 35, for half its appraised value. The Fund then contributed the proceeds from the sale to MROSD's purchase of a second adjacent parcel of 250 acres. Both properties were added to the Long Ridge Open Space Preserve. The "Skyline-to-the-Sea Trail" and the Bay Area Ridge trail converge at this strategic location and the cooperation of these conservation organizations was an indication of the importance of partnerships.

Returning to the completion of Big Basin, in the fall of 1991, the Sempervirens Fund initiated a campaign targeting four key parcels which it called the "Redwood Mosaic" because "each of these missing pieces is an integral part of the seamless panorama of Big Basin". One thirty acre parcel contained a picturesque horse camp, and five years earlier, the Fund had prevented logging on it by purchasing the timber rights through a conservation easement. Another four acre parcel surrounded by parkland was located near the entrance to Big Basin Redwoods State Park. The east fork of the Waddell flows through

a third parcel of ten acres. Funds from the campaign would also be used for a conservation easement to stop logging and permanently protect the ninety acre Blooms Creek Grove. The Fund's share of the $414,000 was added to matching funds from the State to purchase the properties.

In 1991, Fund Executive Director Clausen wrote in *The Mountain Echo* that "(t)he close working ties between the Club — and now the Fund — with the parks department have weathered war, survived the Great Depression, and flourished in boom times. Now we're facing what may be an unprecedented strain: the state budget crisis will likely mean a $30 million cut-back to the state park system". While suggestions for dealing with the shortfall included higher fees and even park closures, Clausen assured his readers that "even in the midst of this funding emergency, we at the Sempervirens Fund are renewing our resolve to preserve nature lands and wildlife in the urban-adjacent wilderness of the Santa Cruz Mountains". As a form of encouragement, the Sequoia Circle was established to honor donors who have given $1,000 or more to Sempervirens Fund campaigns.

In 1992, seventy years after Andrew Hill traveled into the "primeval forest" of Butano to investigate the possibility of adding it to the state park, the Sempervirens Fund embarked on a challenging campaign to purchase the 491 acre Butano Crossing property. The parcel was located high up on the eastern border of Butano Park at the top of the Butano and Gazos Creek watersheds. Butano State Park would now be within the Fund's sphere of influence for the first time. The new acquisition would permit a trail between the two parks, which are separated by less than three miles, and would serve as an important protected corridor for wildlife. The marbled murrelet uses the Butano Crossing as a flyway, and law suits had been filed by the Sierra Club, Earth First, and Greenpeace against Big Creek Lumber Company, owner of the surrounding property, to halt timber cutting on the nearby Butano Ridge. To raise the $1.36 million purchase price, the Fund went into partnership once again with the State and the Save-the-Redwoods League. A $5,000 grant from the Walter and Elise Haas Fund helped to make the campaign a success.

In 1993, the Fund switched its focus from Butano and Big Basin to Castle Rock, and set its sights on buying Upper Fat Buck Ridge, forty-two steep acres of oak and madrone surrounded by park land along Castle Rock's eastern boundary above the headwaters of the San Lorenzo River. With the assistance of the State and the Varian and Packard foundations, the purchase came in time to celebrate the park's 25th anniversary. The ridge was designated as the site of a memorial grove to honor Sempervirens Fund founder Dorothy Varian who had died the year before. A series of Silver Anniversary hikes took place in Castle Rock and a special celebration to mark twenty-five years of the Sempervirens Fund was held in Big Basin Redwoods State Park. The Berry Creek Ridge Nature Trail Exhibit was dedicated, and guests were entertained after a picnic lunch with a "rap history" of the Sempervirens Fund. After announcing that over 7,000 acres — now worth $25 million — had been added to area parks since 1968 through the efforts of the Fund, Executive Director Clausen predicted that in years to come the Sempervirens Fund would remain the prime protector of the Santa Cruz Mountains. "We're committed to safeguarding more precious redwoods, ridge lines, creeks, and watersheds for future generations", he said.

In 1994, the Sempervirens Fund made use of Opportunity Funds, contributions designed to be used for critical opportunities that demand fast action, on two parcels for Big Basin. The Fund acquired full ownership of Trays Ranch, 119 acres along China Grade on the northern border of Big Basin. The following year, a trail was opened not far from the ranch between Big Basin and Pescadero Creek County Park with connections to Portola State Park. The trail was made possible by an easement granted by the owners of the land, Redtree Properties, which permitted horse and hiking access. The Fund assisted the Save-the-Redwoods League in purchasing a 415 acre parcel along the San Lorenzo River containing old-growth redwoods which had been used as a camp for employees of the University of California. A grant of $81,000 from the Jeangerard Foundation allowed for an upgrade of the visitor facilities at Big Basin. All of these efforts were helped by the 135 members in the Fund's Sequoia Circle who had given gifts totaling $328,000.

"Watershed protection", Clausen told a newspaper in 1995, "is the only way to assure long-term protection of parks in state lands, and the integrity of an ecological system." Having secured much, but not all, of the Waddell Creek watershed for Big Basin, the Sempervirens Fund looked north to the Gazos Creek watershed between Big Basin and Butano. An opportunity to buy a large portion of the Gazos Creek Forest presented itself, and the Fund acted quickly by using money from the Opportunity Fund for a $219,500 down payment. One of the six family members who had inherited the property had approached the Sempervirens Fund. When not all of the owners could agree on the sale, the Fund purchased three of the six interests. Then once again, the Sempervirens Fund launched a record-setting campaign, this time to finance the purchase of almost 900 acres of redwoods at a cost of $3.5 million. The campaign lasted three years and was made successful through contributions from the State, the Bradford Foundation, the Packard Foundation, the Save-the-Redwoods League, and individual donors. Ultimately, the Fund took title to a 431 acre parcel along Gazos Creek and another 389 acre parcel of remote redwood forest upstream, both on the southern border of Butano State Park. Of the $1.8 million raised by supporters of the Sempervirens Fund, the smallest gift from an individual was less than one dollar and the largest was $200,000. The average individual gift was $112.58. The Fund had also received $400,000 from the Land and Water Conservation Fund (LWCF), which was established in 1964 to collect taxes on offshore oil drilling and utilize the money to acquire public lands. With this major purchase secured, the Sempervirens Fund had to look no farther than next door for its next purchase. An agreement was signed to buy the former Chuck Taylor Mountain Camp on the border of the Gazos Creek Forest property. The 120 acre camp had been operated for years by Taylor, a former All-American football player and coach, and was purchased for $1.45 million. Resources for this purchase came from California Department of Fish and Game; and from the Gabilan Foundation which contributed $400,000, one of the largest single gifts in Fund history. Additional money came from the Apex Houston Trustee Council, a group established to manage reparation funds for an oil spill from a tanker in 1986 that killed approximately 9,000 sea birds from San Francisco to Long Beach. The Sempervirens

Fund worked closely with the Department of Fish and Game who were members of the Apex Council. Apex would grant the Fund $500,000 for land acquisition and $60,000 for research on the marbled murrelet. The Chuck Taylor Mountain Camp will prove to be an ideal location for a trailhead into the Gazos Creek area.

In the closing years of the 20th century, the Sempervirens Fund continued to connect parks in the Santa Cruz Mountains. In 1997, the Fund engineered a forty-one acre land purchase for $85,000, which linked Big Basin Redwoods State Park and Año Nuevo State Reserve. The State provided $15,000 of the purchase price. The new Whitehouse Ridge Trail, constructed at a cost of $10,000 by a crew from the California Conservation Corps, opened the next summer. It connected two park districts and two counties. In 1999, the Fund purchased Saddle Mountain Ranch near the entrance to the park. Renaming it Shadow Mountain, the Fund planned to use it as a location for activities during its centennial celebration in May, 2000. For its final purchase of the century, the Fund used $25,000 of Opportunity Funds for a down payment on a 170 acre forest-covered ridge top adjacent to Portola State Park, its first project in that area. The $800,000 purchase price for "Island Forest" had to be raised by the end of the year.

Clausen announced his retirement in the summer of 1999, looking back on fourteen years of preserving vital watersheds of the San Lorenzo River, Butano Creek, Gazos Creek, Waddell Creek, and Pescadero Creek. He could be proud of helping to save 3,300 acres of land valued at $14 million. Clausen noted that what had changed since he joined the Sempervirens Fund in 1985 "is a greater appreciation of the value of fish and wildlife habitat, the importance of preserving biodiversity, and the necessity of protecting entire watersheds. Each parcel we acquire must fit into an overall plan of preserving and restoring the integrity of streams, soils, trees, plants, fish and wildlife as vital components of public enjoyment and public responsibility." He further observed that what had not changed was the Fund's "historic quest to provide redwood forests for public enjoyment and recreation".

After an extensive nationwide search, the Board of Directors of the Sempervirens Fund did not delay in appointing Brian Steen to replace Verlyn Clausen as Executive Director. Steen had been Executive Director of the Big Sur Land Trust for the eighteen years immediately preceding his appointment, and was eminently qualified to take over California's oldest successful land trust. While head of the Big Sur Land Trust, Steen had directed seventy-five land transactions which preserved more than 15,000 acres of coastal property.

As Sempervirens entered its second century, Steen reflected on the foresight of those who preceded him, and vowed to continue the purchase and preservation of lands in the Santa Cruz Mountains, as well as the strong cooperative partnership that had developed with California State Parks. In 2000, the Sempervirens Fund saw the lands they had worked to save since 1900, encircled by urban communities. The Santa Cruz Mountains stand out as the major source of recreation, threatened species habitat, critical protected watershed, and countless other benefits for millions of Californians. With dwindling land purchase opportunities at ever increasing prices, the Sempervirens Fund has its challenge laid out in the new millennium. A hundred years of success is a real indication that they are up to the task.

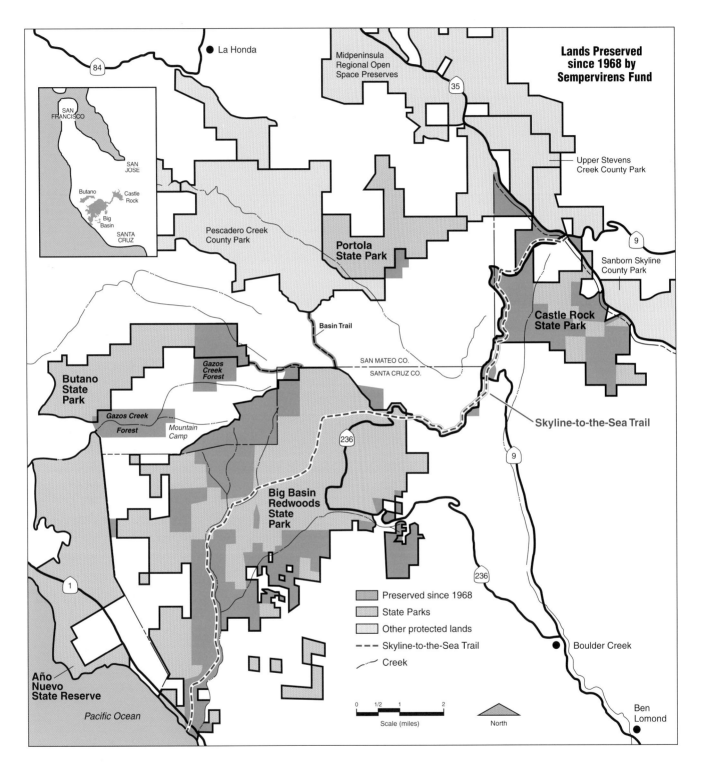

Map of Sempervirens Fund "acquisitions" and the "Skyline-to-the-Sea Trail".     *Source: Sempervirens Fund*

# AFTERWORD
## Moving Forward Into a New Century
### Brian Steen, Executive Director, 1999

The campfire gathering so long ago has produced so much! Lasting land conservation has been achieved over a century by dedicated volunteers, paid professionals, and supported by thousands of people who wanted to help preserve our redwood resources.

However, the vision of a century ago, that of the preservation of all of the redwoods in the Big Basin drainage of the Santa Cruz Mountains is still a distant goal. At this writing, approximately $75 million will be necessary to protect the highest priority properties and virtually none of these lands are for sale at this time. As long as timber and real estate prices continue to rise, few of these properties will be available except to the highest bidder.

The crown jewels of the Santa Cruz Mountains will not be donated; we will have to buy them. Therefore, Sempervirens Fund will have to power up its acquisition and fundraising capabilities in order to compete for increasingly scarce dollars to meet the challenges ahead.

There are very few "good deals" awaiting us. Funding for critical acquisitions will have to, more than ever, come from the private sector. State funds have been historically adequate only after passage of a bond act or an initiative. In all other times, public funds have been scarce or nonexistent. To date, Sempervirens has been helped with funding many State acquisitions, but limited future public funds will necessitate that we help fund maintenance and stewardship of protected lands as well as acquisitions.

To obtain more private sector funding, the Sempervirens Fund plans on expanding its membership base five fold from an active 15,000 present members to at least 75,000 by the year 2010. Our efforts and appeals need to be increasingly shared with the State's and Nation's populations, by presenting our goals and accomplishments using materials and methods that will bring more donors to the cause as regular supporters.

Today's high price will always be tomorrow's bargain. The Sempervirens Fund needs to direct donor support into the area now known as deferred giving, in order to guarantee future funds will be available to purchase key properties. As a tax-deductible nonprofit organization, the Sempervirens Fund can greatly help donors plan their estates to protect future conservation capital, by maximizing tax planning now. Bequests and charitable remainder trusts are powerful tools for donors to direct their future support, thus underwriting Sempervirens' future ability to step forward and make critical land conservation purchases.

In instances where public ownership is not necessary, the Sempervirens Fund plans to encourage private sector land conservation and stewardship on important properties. Carefully worded conservation easements that restrict a property's development and timber rights, are currently the most effective tool available to accomplish long term conservation on private lands. Easements dedicated in perpetuity are tax deductible and, can be used as a powerful estate planning tool.

Working with other conservation groups and public agencies, has brought the redwood preservation movement many successes. The Sempervirens Fund is the principal organization that will continue preserving Santa Cruz Mountain redwood, and other open space lands, for public benefit in the next century. These conservation efforts have always brought together diverse interests. That base of cooperation will have to be greatly expanded to establish new relations with the private business sector, academic institutions, individuals and foundations more than ever, if we are to compete with the real estate and timber industries.

Hickory Oaks, Pine Mountain in background.   *Photo: Kathleen Lyons, Private Collection*

Involving more people requires education and activities to be made available for all ages. The Sempervirens Fund skillfully rode the first wave of environmentalism in the late 1960's and 1970's to involve and educate thousands about the need for land conservation and, the dangers of over-development and commercial logging. The individuals and groups that learned those lessons a generation ago are today's community and conservation leaders. The future leaders of the land preservation movement must represent business and community interests in a much broader manner, than those purely traditional conservation-oriented organizations. Land conservation should and can become relevant to people in all walks of life.

In the 1980's, the Sempervirens Fund greatly expanded its membership and donor support as it purchased threatened properties. With much of its time devoted to the technical matters associated with land preservation, educational programs were minimal although effective.

Moving forward to continue past success requires a revised and ambitious education program for all ages. Taking advantage of the Internet and other media communications technology is just the beginning, and can be our most leveraged form of communication and education. At the same time we must not lose the personal interaction which has been and will be always most important.

Environmental education in the classroom and in the forest should be promoted and implemented on a scheduled basis. Special outings, trail hikes, and other activities should be regularly planned as primary social activities for the Sempervirens Fund to invite and involve new supporters.

The public's increasing need to escape escalating urbanization has also been a century in developing. We must recognize that as the population pressures increase, impacts on our natural resources will become even greater.

To preserve those limited lands for public benefit will require more action and less talk; more commitment and less compromise; a new vision and creative solutions to be implemented. We pledge the land conservation results for the next century will be equal to or even better than the results of the hard work of the past 100 years.

The journey will be challenging and costly but infinitely worth the effort.

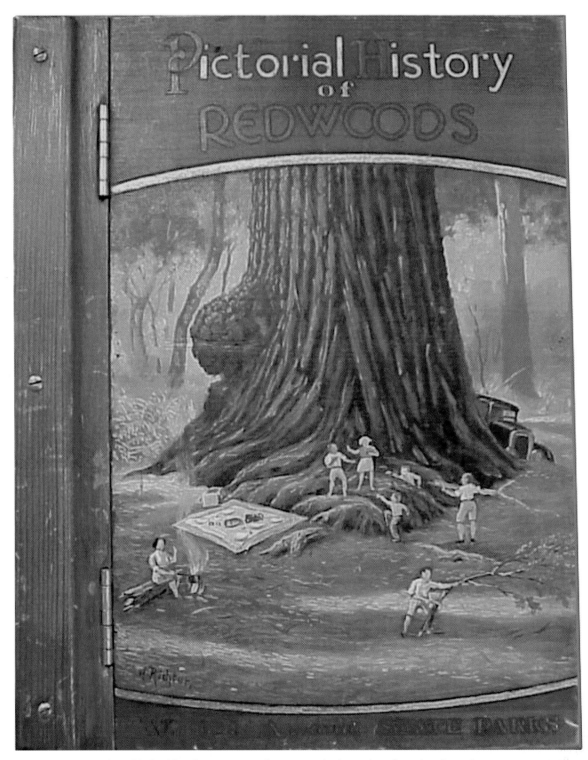

Book published by the W.P.A. and State Parks bound with real redwood covers.
*Photo: Courtesy, History San Jose Collection*

# Bibliography

Abbott, Jr., Gordon. *Saving Special Places: A Centennial History of The Trustees of Reservations: Pioneer of the Land Trust Movement*. Ipswitch, MA: The Ipswitch Press, 1993.

Albee, Wilson E. "The Attractions of the Big Basin, or California Redwood Park", reprinted in Eugene T. Sawyer, *History of Santa Clara County, 1922*. Chapter XX, 206-210; reprint of article from *San Jose Mercury*, April 22, 1917. No publisher.

Arbuckle, Helen. "Carrie Stevens Walter", *Trailblazer*, 39:2, June, 1998.

Bakker, Elna. *An Island Called California: An Ecological Introduction to its Natural Communities*. Berkeley and Los Angeles: University of California Press, 1971.

Barrett, Thomas S., and Putnam Livermore. *The Conservation Easement in California*. Covelo, CA: Island Press, 1983.

Bergazzi, Michael. "Santa Cruz County Lumbering", transcript of interview conducted by Elizabeth Spedding Calciano, 1964, University of California, Santa Cruz, Special Collections.

Berger, John J. "Redwoods Rising" in *Restoring the Earth: How Americans are Working to Renew Our Damaged Environment*, 69-78. New York: Alfred A. Knopf, 1985.

_____. "Trees and a Man: Tony Look's Dream Rescues an Ecosystem", *Sierra*, November/December 1979, 34-38.

Brown, Alan K., and Frank M. Stanger. "Discovery of the Redwoods", *Forest History*, XIII, October 1969, 6-11.

Brown, Alan K. *Sawpits in the Spanish Redwoods, 1789-1849*. San Mateo: San Mateo County Historical Association, 1966.

Burgess, Sherwood D. "Lumbering in Hispanic California". *California Historical Society Quarterly* XLI, no. 3, September, 1962, 237-248.

Clar, C. Raymond. *California Government and Forestry: From Spanish Days Until the Creation of the Department of Natural Resources in 1927*. Sacramento: Dept. of Natural Resources, 1959.

Clark, Donald Thomas. *Santa Cruz County Place Names: A Geographical Dictionary*. Santa Cruz: Santa Cruz Historical Society, 1986.

Clark, F.L. "The Big Basin", *Sierra Club Bulletin*, III, February 1901, 218-223.

Cohen, Michael P. *The History of the Sierra Club, 1892-1970*. San Francisco: Sierra Club Books, 1988.

Colburn, Frona Eunice Wait. "Mrs. Lovell White — As I Knew Her", *Overland Monthly* and *Out West Magazine*, 81:6, October 1923.

Coolbaugh, Joel W. "The Sawmill Era: A History of the Redwood Industry in Santa Cruz County", unpublished paper, University of California, Santa Cruz, Special Collections, 1963.

Curtis, James R.. "New Chicago of the Far West: Land Speculation in Alvison, California, 1890-1891", *California Historical Quarterly*, LXI:1, Spring 1982, 36-45.

Dasmann, Raymond F. *The Destruction of California*. New York: Macmillan, 1965.

Delmas, D.M. "Address Before the Legislature 18th of February, 1901", in *Speeches and Addresses*. San Francisco: A. M. Robertson, 1901, 353-363.

Deverell, William. *Railroad Crossing: Californians and the Railroad, 1850-1910*. Berkeley and Los Angeles: University of California Press, 1994.

De Vries, Carolyn. *Grand and Ancient Forest: The Story of Andrew P. Hill and Big Basin Redwood State Park*. Fresno: Valley Publishers, 1978.

Dudley, William R. "The Big Basin", *The Stanford Sequoia*, X:17, April 16, 1901, 362-366.

_____. "The Big Basin: A Legacy of the Ages", *Palo Alto Live Oak*, April/May 1901, 1-4.

_____. "The Big Basin Redwood Park", *Forester*, VII, July 1901, 157-164.

_____. "The Redwood Reservation Act", *Sierra Club Bulletin*, III, June 1901, 337-338.

Duzet, Harriet. "Carrie Stevens Walter: Writer, Poet, Nature Lover, Mother", *Argonauts*, Jan. & Feb., 1995.

Elliott, W.W. *Santa Cruz County, California. Illustrations, with Historical Sketch of the County*. San Francisco: Wallace W. Elliott & Co., 1879; reprinted by Santa Cruz Museum of Art and History, 1997.

Ellsworth, Rodney S. "Historical Sketch of the Maddock Family", in *Pictorial History of the Redwoods*, vol. 1. Sacramento: Department of Parks and Recreation, c.1930.

Engbeck, Joseph H., Jr. *The Enduring Giants*. Berkeley: University Extension, University of California, 1973.

_____. *State Parks of California: from 1864 to the Present*. San Francisco: Belding, 1980.

Fox, Stephen. *The American Conservation Movement: John Muir and His Legacy*. Madison: University of Wisconsin, 1985.

French, Harold. "A Pedestrian's Paseaur in the Big Basin", *Overland Monthly*, XLX, February 1905, 89-96.

Fuller, David W. "Vallco Park: From Orchards to Industry", in *Seconaid*, L. McArthur and David W. Fuller, eds., *Cupertino Chronicle*. Cupertino: California History Center, De Anza College, 1975.

Fulmer, F.R. "Roy". *General Information on Big Basin Redwood Trees and California Redwood Park*. Santa Cruz, c.1925.

Gelber, Gertrude Johansen. "The Johansen Family and the Hollow Tree Camp Shingle Mill", privately printed, Santa Cruz History Museum collection, 1972.

Gibson, Mary S. *A Record of Twenty-Five Years of the California Federation of Women's Clubs, 1900-1925: A Handbook for Clubwomen*. California Federation of Women's Clubs, 1927.

Gordon, Burton L. *Monterey Bay Area: Natural History and Cultural Imprints*. Pacific Grove, Calif.: Boxwood Press, 1985.

Greenlee, Jason. "Vegetation, Fire History and Fire Potential of Big Basin Redwoods State Park, California", unpublished Ph.D. thesis, University of California, Santa Cruz, 1983.

Gross, Frances. "A Queen of Clubs", *Sunset*, 28:5, May 1912, 597-599.

Guinn, James Miller. *History of the State of California and Biographic Record of Santa Cruz...Counties*. Chicago: Chapman Publishing, 1903.

Hague, Harlan, and David J. Langum. *Thomas O. Larkin: A Life of Patriotism and Profit in Old California*. Norman and London: University of Oklahoma, 1990.

Hall, Austin. *Unto the Children: A Story of the Redwoods*. San Jose: Semperviren's Club of California, 1924.

Hamman, Rick. *California Central Coast Railways*. Boulder, Co.: Pruett Publishing, 1980.

Harrison, Edward Sanford. *History of Santa Cruz County, California*. San Francisco: Pacific Press Publishing Company, 1892.

Hays, Samuel. *Conservation and the Gospel of Efficiency: The Progressive Conservation Movement, 1890-1920*. Cambridge, MA: Harvard University Press, 1959.

Hecht, Barry, and Barbara Rushmore, ed. *Waddell Creek: The Environment around Big Basin, Santa Cruz Mountains, California*. Santa Cruz: University of California, Santa Cruz, Environmental Studies, and Sempervirens Fund, 1972.

Hichborn, Franklin, with introduction by Herbert Jones. "The Party, the Machine, and the Vote: The Story of Cross Filing in California Politics", *California Historical Society Quarterly*, XXXVIII:4, Dec. 1959, 349-351.

Hill, Frank E., and Florence W. Hill. *The Acquisition of California Redwood Park*. San Jose, 1927.

Hocker, Jean. "Good-guy Real Estate (Land Trust Alliance)", *Whole Earth 94*, Fall 1998, 41-42.

Holder, C.F. "How a Forest Fire was Extinguished with Wine", with photographs by Andrew Hill, *The Wide World Magazine*, V:28, July 1900, 339-348.

Hoover, Mildred (Brooke). *Historic Spots in California: Counties of the Coast Range*. Stanford: Stanford University Press, 1937; 3rd ed., 1966.

Houston, James. "Delphin Delmas", in *A Centennial History of the Sainte Claire Club, 1888-1988*. Cupertino: California History Center Foundation, 1988.

Hyde, Anne Farrar. "William Kent: The Puzzle of Progressive Conservationists", in *California Progressivism Revisited*, ed. William Deverell and Tom Sitton. Berkeley and Los Angeles: University of California Press, 1994.

Ise, John. *Our National Park Policy: A Critical History*. Baltimore: Johns Hopkins Press, 1961.

Jamieson, Allen. "Big Basin and Castle Rock", *Sierra Club Bulletin*, September 1968, 12-18.

Johnston, Verna R. "Redwood Forests", in *California Forests and Woodlands: A Natural History*. Berkeley: University of California Press, 1994.

Jones, Douglas. "King of the Forest", *Modern Maturity*, August/September 1982, 38.

Jones, Holway R. *John Muir and the Sierra Club: The Battle for Yosemite*. San Francisco: Sierra Club, 1965.

Jones, Louise (Mrs. Stephen A.). "The Sequoia Sempervirens, or Coast Redwood of California", *Arboriculture*, II:4, May, 1903, 184-192.

Koch, Margaret. *Santa Cruz County: Parade of the Past*. Fresno, CA: Valley Publishers, 1973.

Leonard, Richard M. "Mountaineer, Lawyer, Environmentalist", oral history conducted by Susan R. Schrepfer for Regional Oral History Office, University of California, 1975. Includes interview with Doris Leonard.

Look, Claude A. "Sempervirens Fund: An Evergreen Conservation Effort", *Fremontia*, October 1979, 28-29.

Lyons, Kathleen, and Mary Beth Cooney-Lazaneo. *Plants of the Coast Redwood Region*. Boulder Creek, CA: Looking Press, 1988.

Margolin, Malcolm. *The Ohlone Way: Indian Life in the San Francisco-Monterey Bay Area*. Berkeley, CA: Heydey Books, 1978.

Mars, Amaury. *Reminiscences of Santa Clara Valley and San Jose*. San Francisco: Mysell-Rollins Co., 1901.

Massmann, Priscilla G. "A Neglected Partnership: The General Federation of Women's Clubs and the Conservation Movement, 1890-1920", Ph.D. dissertation, University of Connecticut, 1997.

McCarthy, Nancy. *Where Grizzlies Roamed the Canyons: The Story of the San Lorenzo Valley*. Palo Alto: Garden Court Press, 1994.

McCrackin, Josephine Clifford. "About the Big Basin", *Overland Monthly*, August 1900, 135-139.

_____. "How the Big Basin Redwoods were Saved", *Out West*, XX, 1904, 35-44.

_____. "In the Heart of the Big Basin with the Sempervirens Club", *Western Field Magazine*, November 1904, 185-192.

McLean, Hulda Hoover. "A History of Rancho Del Oso", *News and Notes from the Santa Cruz Historical Society*, XLVIII, June 1971, 1-6.

_____. "Rancho del Oso, How It Was, 1914-1946", *Santa Cruz County History Journal*, 1, 1994, 61-66.

Meadows, Donald. "A Manual of the History and Biology of the Big Basin Redwoods State Park, California", unpublished paper, 1950.

Melendy, H.B. "One Hundred Years of the Redwood Lumber Industry, 1850-1950", doctoral dissertation, Stanford University.

Merchant, Carolyn. "Women of the Progressive Conservation Movement: 1900-1916", *Environmental Review*, 8, no. 1, Spring 1984, 57-85.

Merchant, Carolyn, ed. *Green Versus Gold: Sources in California's Environmental History*. Washington, D.C.: Island Press, 1998.

Meuser, Michael R. "Appearances of Nature and Local Environmental Politics: the Forest of Nisene Marks, Santa Cruz County, California", M.A. thesis, University of California, Santa Cruz, 1994.

Milliken, Randall. *A Time of Little Choice: The Disintegration of Tribal Culture in the San Francisco Bay Area, 1769-1810*. Menlo Park, CA: Ballena Press, 1995.

Mori, Christine. "The Redwood Forest and Santa Cruz Lumbering", University of California, Santa Cruz, Library Special Collections, 1971.

Morton, Don. "Big Basin Redwoods (California Redwood Park), State Park No. 38", in *History of California State Parks*, ed. by Vernon Aubrey Neasham. State of California, Department of Natural Resources, Div. of Parks, 1937.

O'Day, Edward, and F. O'Day. "Laura White", in *Varied Types*. Town Talk Press, 1915.

Palmer, Tim. *California's Threatened Environment: Restoring the Dream*. Washington, D.C.: Island Press, 1993.

Payne, Stephen. *A Howling Wilderness: The Summit Road of the Santa Cruz Mountains 1850-1906*. Los Gatos, CA: Loma Prieta Publishing, 1978.

Peyton, West. "The Man Who Led the Fight for the Valley's Water Hole", in *San Jose: A Personal View*, San Jose Historical Museum Association, 1989, 3-6.

Poole, William. "In Land We Trust", *Sierra*, 77:2, March-April, 1992, 52.

Posner, Russell. "The Progressive Voters League, 1923-26", *California Historical Society Quarterly*, 36:3, September 1957, 251-261.

Rawls, James J., and Walton Bean. *California: An Interpretive History*. New York: McGraw-Hill, 6th ed., 1993.

Reed, Charles Wesley, and Carrie Stevens Walter. *Save the California Redwoods: "Woodman Spare That Tree"*. San Francisco: Sempervirens Club, 1900.

Rice, Bertha, M. *Builders of Our Valley*, vol. 1. San Jose: 1957.

_____. *The Women of Our Valley*. San Jose: 1955.

Richards, Don W. Music by Thomas V. Cator. *The Soul of Sequoia: A Forest Play*. San Jose: Sempervirens Club of California, 1919.

Richards, W.W. "The Redwood Park in the Big Basin a Game Preserve", *San Jose Daily Mercury*, Nov. 24, 1901, 9.

_____. "Visiting Big Basin: San Joseans View Its Splendid Trees", *San Jose Evening News*, May 16, 1900.

Richardson, R. Randolph. "Steward Little: Which Land Trusts Can You Trust?", in *Policy Review 74*, Fall 1995, 87-88.

Robinson, William Condit. "The Historical Geography of the Redwood Forests of the Santa Cruz Mountains", Ph.D. dissertation, University of California, Berkeley, 1949.

Rood, Robert C. "The Historical Geography and Environmental Impact of the Lumber Industry of the Santa Cruz Mountains", University of California, Santa Cruz, Special Collections, 1975.

Roorbach, Eloise J. "The Big Basin", *Overland Monthly*, October 1907, 301-308.

Rowland, Leon. *Santa Cruz: The Early Years*. Santa Cruz, CA: Paper Vision Press, 1980.

Rushmore, Jean. *The Bay Area Ridge Trail: Ridgetop Adventures Above San Francisco Bay*. Berkeley: Wilderness Press, 1995.

Sawyer, Eugene Taylor. *History of Santa Clara County*. Los Angeles: Historic Record Co., 1922.

Schrepfer, Susan R. *The Fight to Save the Redwoods: A History of Environmental Reform 1917-1978*. Madison: University of Wisconsin, 1983.

Shon, Lisa, and D.W. Gotthold. "History and bibliography concerning the Waddell Creek Basin", Santa Cruz County, unpublished paper, 1970.

Singer, Steven W., and Denzil Verardo. "The Murrelet's Nest Discovered", *Pacific Discovery*, XXVIII, August, 1975, pp. 18-22.

Smith, Michael L. *Pacific Visions: California Scientists and the Environment,1850-1915*. New Haven and London: Yale University Press, 1987.

Smith, Ralph Sidney. "The Redwood Reserve Plan: A plan to save portions of the Coast Redwood Forest", Bancroft Library collection, n.d.

Stanford, Everett Russell. "A Short History of California Lumbering", Masters thesis, University of California, Berkeley, 1923.

Stanger, Frank M. *Sawmills in the Redwoods: Logging on the San Francisco Peninsula 1849-1967*. San Mateo, CA: San Mateo County Historical Association, 1967.

Starr, Kevin. *Americans and the California Dream, 1850-1915*. New York: Oxford University Press, 1973.

Stevens, Stanley D. "History of the 1912 'Map of California Redwood Park: The Big Basin'", Santa Cruz, unpublished paper, 1994.

Stillman, Albert. "How the Big Basin Was Saved", *Touring Topics*, Jan. 1902, 26-27.

Taber, Tom. *The Santa Cruz Mountains Trail Book*. 6th edition. Oak Valley Press, 1991.

Taylor, Arthur A. *California Redwood Park: Sometimes Called Sempervirens Park: An Appreciation*. Sacramento, 1912.

Temple, Edwin O'Brian. "From Lumbering to Horticulture", *Overland Monthly*, January 1902, 579-594.

Thomson, Jeff. *The Forest of Nisene Marks State Park*. Soquel: Walkabout Publications, 1995.

Tilden, Freeman. *The State Parks: Their Meaning in American Life*. New York: Knopf, 1962.

Turner, Frederick. *Rediscovering America: John Muir in His Time and Ours*. San Francisco: Sierra Club Books, 1985.

Verardo, Denzil, and Alexander Lowry. *Big Basin*. Los Altos, CA: Sempervirens Fund, 1973.

Verardo, Jennie and Denzil Verardo. *Restless Paradise: Santa Cruz County. An Illustrated History*. Northridge, CA: Windsor Publications, 1987.

Walter, Carrie Stevens. "The Preservation of the Big Basin", *Overland Monthly*, October 1902, 354-358.

_____. "From San Francisco to Santa Cruz", *The Golden Era*, May 1886, 281-287.

_____. *Rose-Ashes*. C. A. Murdock, 1890; republished as *Rose Ashes and other Poems*, San Jose: A.C. Eaton, 1907.

_____. "Saving the Big Basin", *San Francisco Chronicle*, May 27, 1900, 32.

_____. "True History of the Big Basin Movement", *San Jose Herald*, Aug. 9, 1901.

Waters, Donald A. "Billy Dool — a BC Pioneer who helped preserve Big Basin Area", *The Valley Press*, Feb. 16, 1977, 11.

Waters, Don. "Notes from a Son of the Forest", *The Santa Cruz Weekly*, Nov. 26-Dec. 2, 1980, 13-15.

Wattenburger, Ralph. "The Redwood Lumbering Industry in the Northern California Coast, 1850-1900", M.A. thesis, University of California, Berkeley, 1931.

Weaver, Harriett. "Andrew Hill, He Saved the Redwoods", *Westways*, January 1954, 25.

Wilson, Richard C. "Early Day Lumber Operations in the Santa Cruz Redwood Region", *The Timberman*, May 1937.

_____. "Redwoods of the Santa Cruz—A Logging Saga", *American Forests*, October, 1937, 478-511.

Wood, Mary I. *The History of the General Federal of Women's Clubs for the First Twenty-two Years*. Unk.: 1912.

Hickory Oaks.     *Photo: Sempervirens Fund Collection*

1900.
1927.

This album is presented to the

Sempervirens Club of California

at their twenty seventh reunion

California Redwood Park

Big Basin, Santa Cruz County

Where: twenty seven years ago, eight charter members formed the club for the purpose of saving and preserving this magnificent grove of Sequoia Sempervirens trees, for posterity, and the glory of California.

These beautiful photographs were all taken by our fellow member, and dear friend Andrew P. Hill, Father of Sempervirens Club

H. H. Richards.
a Charter Member.

First page in a photo album of Andrew Hill's work presented to the Sempervirens Club on their 27th anniversary.

*Photo: Courtesy, History San Jose Collection*

# Appendix
## Sempervirens' Presidents

### Sempervirens Club

| | |
|---|---|
| Charles Wesley Reed | 1900 — 1903 |
| Laura White | 1903 — 1906 |
| Rev. Eli McClish | 1906 — 1907 |
| Kate Moody Kennedy | 1907 — 1908 |
| Andrew P. Hill | 1908 — 1922 |
| Alexander Murgotten | 1922 — 1923 |
| S.W. Waterhouse | 1923 — 1923 |
| William Flint | 1923 — 1926 |
| Wallace Isham | 1926 — 1945 |
| Herbert Jones | 1945 — 1968 |

### Sempervirens Fund of Conservation Associates

| | |
|---|---|
| George Collins | 1968 — 1971 |

### Sempervirens Fund

| | |
|---|---|
| George Collins | 1971 — 1972 |
| Richard P. Wheat, M.D. | 1972 — 1983 |
| John R. Burgis | 1983 — 1986 |
| Richard P. Wheat, M.D. | 1986 — 1988 |
| Dunham Sherer | 1988 — 1993 |
| Mary Davey | 1993 — 1995 |
| Ellen C. Weaver | 1995 — 1998 |
| John Luckhardt | 1998 — |

### Sempervirens Fund Executive Directors

| | |
|---|---|
| Claude A. "Tony" Look | 1971 — 1985 |
| Verlyn H. Clausen | 1985 — 1999 |
| Brian L. Steen | 1999 — |

### 2000 Board of Directors

| | |
|---|---|
| John D. Luckhardt, President | Michael S. Barton, Vice President |
| Betsy B. Ross, Secretary | Geza L. Gyorey, Treasurer |
| Robert A. Bryan | William N. Harris |
| Gil V. Hernandez | Claude A. "Tony" Look |
| Doti Sherer | Richard P. Wheat, M.D. |
| Stephen N. Wyckoff | |
| | |
| Howard J. King | Honorary Vice President |
| Thomas K. McCarthy | Honorary Vice President |

| **Executive Director** | **Director of Development** |
|---|---|
| Brian L. Steen | John Gilliland |

Early chartered auto tour to Big Basin Redwoods State Park. *Photo: Andrew P. Hill, Sempervirens Fund Collection*

# Author Biographies

### Willie Yaryan

Willie Yaryan lives among the redwoods in the Santa Cruz Mountains with his wife, Cici, and their nearly-grown children, Molly and Nick. After many careers including journalism, entertainment public relations, and magazine publishing, he settled down in academia where he is writing a Ph.D. dissertation in environmental history at the University of California at Santa Cruz on the ideology and political economy of nature preservation with Big Basin as a case study.

### Denzil and Jennie Verardo

Denzil and Jennie Verardo, both natives of the Salinas Valley, have been writing history together for over 28 years. Denzil holds a B.A. in history from the University of California at Santa Cruz. He also has an M.A. in history, and a Doctoral Degree in Management. Denzil Verardo has been employed by the California Department of Parks and Recreation for the past 28 years, and currently serves as the Department's Chief Deputy Director, Administrative Services.

Also a graduate of the University of California, Santa Cruz, Jennie holds an M.P.A. from Golden Gate University and works for the California Conservation Corps as Manager of its Recruitment and Corpsmember Development Programs. Jennie and Denzil are both Sponsors of the Sempervirens Fund and were charter members. They have written and lectured extensively on the history of California State Parks as well as having authored seven other books. They have published more than 200 articles on a variety of topics, and have received numerous awards and commendations for their work.

*Design and Production: Dick Teater*
*Production Editing: Kit Teater*
*Composed in Linotype-Hell AG Cochin*
*at Teater & etc., Mountain View, California*

*Color & B/W Photo Scans by:*
*CBM Type, Sunnyvale, California*

*Printed & Bound by:*
*Commerce Printing Service, Sacramento, California*
*on Endeavour Velvet Cover and Book*